Presented to

Orson Alder Woodall

From

Trinity Lutheran Church
of Minnehaha Falls

On

Your Baptism
June 24, 2007

DAVID C. COOK

CHILDREN'S
BIBLE
STORY BOOK

Faith Kidz® is an imprint of
Cook Communications Ministries, Colorado Springs, CO 80918
Cook Communications, Paris, Ontario
Kingsway Communications, Eastbourne, England

David C. Cook Children's Bible Story Book
© 2006 by Cook Communications Ministries for text and art

Cover design by: BMB Design
Interior design by: Granite Design
Illustrations by: Richard Williams

First Printing, 2006
Printed in Thailand

1 2 3 4 5 6 7 8 9 10 Printing/Year 10 09 08 07 06

ISBN: 978-0-7814-4386-9

Contents

Old Testament

God Makes Day and Night 10
God Makes Plants 12
God Makes All Kinds of Animals 14
God Makes People Special 18
Adam and Eve Sin 20
Cain and Abel Fight 22
God Cares for Noah 26
Noah Shows Love to God 30
God Calls Abraham 34
Abraham and Lot Part Company 38
Lot Leaves Town 42
God Keeps His Promise to Abraham 44
God Tests Abraham 46
Isaac Gets a Wife 48
Isaac's Neighbors Pick a Fight 50
Jacob Tricks His Father 54
Jacob and Esau Forgive 56
Joseph's Brothers Tell a Lie 60
Joseph Helps Pharaoh 62
Joseph Forgives His Brothers 66
God Protects Baby Moses 70
Moses Sees a Burning Bush 72
Moses and Aaron Talk to Pharaoh 74
God's People Obey 78
Moses Parts the Red Sea 82
God Gives Water to His People 86
Moses Listens to Good Advice 90
Aaron Builds a Golden Calf 92
God Gives the Ten Commandments 94
God's People Give Their Talents 96
The Walls of Jericho Fall 98
God Chooses Gideon 102

Gideon Wins the Battle 106

Hannah Asks God for a Child 110

God Chooses Saul to Be King 114

Saul Disobeys God 116

David Fights a Giant 118

David Helps Saul 122

David and Jonathan Become Friends 124

David Spares Saul's Life 128

David Dances 132

Solomon Chooses Wisdom 134

Solomon Uses God's Wisdom 138

Solomon Follows God's Plan for the Temple 142

Solomon Worships God with Prayer 146

Elijah Sees God's Power 148

Elijah Hears God's Voice 152

Elijah Is Taken to Heaven 156

Elisha's Servant Sees Angels 160

Josiah Listens to God's Word 164

Jehoshaphat Fights God's Way 168

Joash and the People Worship God with Gifts 170

King Hezekiah and the People Worship God with Music 174

Ezra Rebuilds the Temple 178

Esther Takes a Stand 180

Job Suffers 184

God Calls Isaiah 186

God's Word Burns Up 190

Daniel Eats Vegetables 192

Three Men Survive a Fiery Furnace 194

A Hand Writes on a Wall 198

Daniel Lives with Lions 200

Love God First 204

Jonah Swims with a Fish 208

New Testament

An Angel Visits Mary 214
An Angel Visits Joseph 216
Joseph and Mary Welcome Baby Jesus 218
Angels and Shepherds Tell Good News 222
Simeon Blesses Jesus 226
Wise Men Worship Jesus 228
God Takes Care of Jesus 230
Jesus Gets "Lost" 232
John Baptizes Jesus 236
Jesus Chooses God's Way 240
Jesus Teaches God's Word 244
Jesus Says, "Follow Me" 246
Jesus Heals a Man with Leprosy 250
Jesus Calls Matthew 254
Jesus Heals on the Sabbath 258
Four Friends Help 260
Nicodemus Comes to Jesus 264
Jesus Meets a Woman at a Well 266
Jesus Heals a Man Who Can't Walk 270
Jesus Chooses His Disciples 274
God Cares for Us 278
Two Men Build Houses 280
Jesus Heals a Little Girl 284
A Boy Shares His Lunch 288
Peter Walks on Water 292
Jesus Heals a Woman's Daughter 296
Jesus Teaches How to Forgive 298
Jesus Spots a Trap 302
Three Men Handle Money 304
God Remembers How We Treat Others 306
Jesus Teaches Prayer 310
Jesus Helps a Man Believe 312
Jesus Is the Good Shepherd 314
Parable of the Rich Man 318
Jesus Tells About Shepherds 322
A Selfish Son Comes Home 326
Jesus Raises Lazarus from the Dead 330

Jesus Loves the Children 334
James and John Want to Be First 336
Jesus Calls Zacchaeus 338
The Most Important Rule 340
Jesus Serves by Washing Feet 342
Jesus Dies 344
Jesus Comes Back to Life! 348
Two Friends Meet a Stranger 352
Jesus Appears to Thomas 354
Jesus Takes Peter Back 356
Jesus Returns to Heaven 360
The Holy Spirit Comes 364
Peter and James Heal a Lame Man 368
Paul Meets Jesus 370
Paul Escapes in a Basket 374
Peter Helps Dorcas 378
Barnabas and Paul Work Together 380
An Angel Frees Peter 382
Paul and Silas Sing in Jail 386
Timothy's Family Helps Him Know God 390
Paul Helps People Know God 394
New Friends Learn About Jesus 396
Paul Cares for the Church 398
Paul's Ship Sinks 400
Paul Teaches About Giving 404
Onesimus Comes Home 406

Indexes
    "To Remember" Verses 408
    Bible Story References 412

OLD TESTAMENT

God Makes Day and Night

I n the very beginning there was God, but nothing else. Then God made the heavens and the earth. The Bible says the earth looked different than it does now because it was completely covered with water. There was no land anywhere, and everything was completely dark! Darkness was everywhere. The darkness you see when you close your eyes is like the total darkness that was all over the earth.

God said, "Let there be light." And there was light. God saw that the light he made was good. He named the light "day." God also gave a name to the darkness. He called it "night." That's how God made day and night during his first day of Creation.

But God wanted more than day and night. He wanted his creation to have many lights. God said, "Let there be lights in the sky." And that's exactly what happened. God made one light for the day and the other for the night: the sun and the moon. And he made the stars.

God made day, night, and the sun, moon, and stars. God saw that all the lights he made were good.

Prayer Point

Try to imagine how dark it was before God made light. How dark can you make your room? The earth was darker than that. It was so dark that even with night vision glasses you couldn't see anything. But God wanted light! Thank you, God, for light.

God Makes Plants

God made all kinds of plants to grow on the earth. He made them to be good for food and pretty to look at.

God made grass—some kinds of grass to grow on hills and mountains, other kinds to grow at the edges of lakes and ponds.

God made the trees. He made trees of all different kinds. Some grow food for animals and people. Trees give animals places to live, and they give us shade and other things we use.

God made flowers to grow in different sizes, shapes, and colors. He made the flowers to smell nice. Some kinds of flowers grow in a lot of water. Others grow where they get only a little water. He made plants that grow in the rocky soil in the mountains and in the dry, sandy deserts.

God made plants that give us good food: fruits, vegetables, and grains.

God looked at the plants he had made. They were beautiful and good. God saw that everything he had made was good.

To Remember

God said, "Let the land produce plants."...And that's exactly what happened.   Genesis 1:11

Did You Know?

There are 250,000 types of trees and plants, over 51,000 types of animals, and at least 500,000 different types of insects. How many kinds of trees, plants, and animals can you name? Make a list and watch it grow every time you think of a new one. Remember, God made all of them!

God Makes All Kinds of Animals

God had made the world. He made all of the plants. But God wasn't finished. Next he made all kinds of animals.

God said, "Let the rivers, lakes, and oceans be filled with animals that live in water." Splash! He made all kinds of water animals—whales, sharks, starfish, crabs, goldfish, and trout.

God also said, "Let birds fly through the sky." God made big birds like eagles and little birds like parakeets. God made some birds to make their nests in the trees. Other kinds of birds make their nests in the grass. God made birds to eat nuts and seeds. The plants that birds would use for food and places for nests were already there because God made everything in order.

God made birds like ducks and penguins to swim in the water. Some birds, like the ostrich, run fast but can't fly. But God made them too.

God saw that all the fish and birds he made were good. But he wasn't finished filling the world he made. God made animals that live on the land. He made giraffes with long necks and elephants with long noses. God made

all the animals, like cows and pigs, that we see when we go to a farm. He made the polar bears that live in cold snowy places and the lions that live in the warm jungles. God made all kinds of animals to live on all the different lands he had made.

God also made all kinds of insects and spiders. He made some kinds of insects to fly and others to hop or crawl. God made the spiders and insects to use the land and plants he made for their food and homes.

After God made all the animals, he saw that they were good.

God gave the animals food and places to live in the wonderful world he made. God made all kinds of animals to fill the world he made.

To Remember

God made all kinds of wild animals. He made all kinds of livestock. He made all kinds of creatures that move along the ground. And God saw that it was good.

Genesis 1:25

Prayer Point

God made every creature on the earth, but we are responsible for taking care of them. What can you do to help them be safe? Thank you, God, for trusting us with your creation.

God Makes People Special

God wasn't finished making all he wanted to put on the earth. What God was going to make next would be his most special creation.

God said, "Let us make people." With these words God made the first man. He named him Adam. God said, "I will make a helper for Adam so he is not alone." God made the first woman. Adam named her Eve.

After God made people he told them to rule over all creation. This means that God made people to be more important than the plants and animals.

God also made us in his likeness. That means we can learn about God, love God, and talk with him. Because we are made in God's likeness, we can choose between right and wrong.

God also made people special by making them able to love each other.

People are the only part of God's creation that can pray and sing to worship him.

God made people different from everything else he created. People are God's special creation.

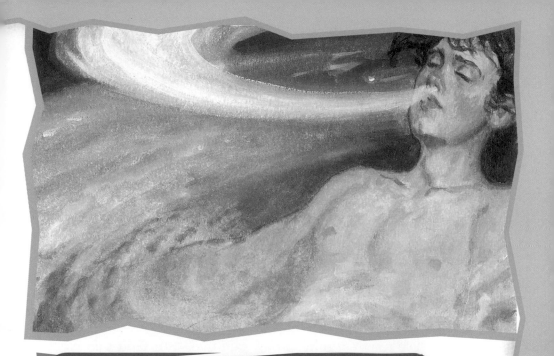

To Remember

Then the Lord God formed a man. He made him out of the dust of the ground. He breathed the breath of life into him. And the man became a living person.   Genesis 2:7

Did You Know?

Everything God made was good. But when he made the first people he loved them more than anything else he had made, and he still does! Did you know you were so special to God? Thank you, God, for loving me more than anything.

Adam and Eve Sin

Adam and Eve lived in a beautiful garden. The trees in the garden had fruit.

God said, "Enjoy the fruit. It is for you. But one tree is special. Do not eat from it. If you do, I will punish you."

Adam and Eve obeyed God. They were happy.

One day Eve was near the special tree, and a snake (Satan) said to her, "Did God say not to eat this fruit?"

"We may eat other fruit," said Eve. "But God said we will be punished if we eat this fruit."

"You won't be punished," said Satan. "You will know good and bad. You will know what God knows."

Eve looked at the tree. The fruit looked so good! She wanted to know everything God knows.

Eve ate some of the fruit. She gave some to Adam. He ate some too.

God came to talk to them. But they hid because they were afraid. They were afraid because they didn't obey.

God said, "You disobeyed. Now there are conse-quences."

God sent Adam and Eve out of the garden. He said,

"You must work hard now. You will not always be happy."

Adam and Eve were sad. They knew they had done wrong. So they left the garden, as God had told them to do, and they had to work for their food from then on.

To Remember

The Lord God gave the man a command. He said, "You can eat the fruit of any tree that is in the garden. But you must not eat the fruit of the tree of the knowledge of good and evil."
Genesis 2:16-17

Cain and Abel Fight

Adam and Eve did not obey God. So they had to go away from the garden. But they did not forget God.

And God still loved them.

Adam and Eve had two boys. One boy's name was Cain.

Cain grew up to be a farmer. He planted grain in the field.

The other boy was Abel. Abel grew up to be a shepherd.

He took care of sheep.

Adam taught the boys to give offerings to God.

Abel wanted to please God. He gave God his best sheep. God was happy with Abel.

Cain gave God some grain from his fields. But Cain didn't care if he pleased God. He did not obey God.

So God did not accept Cain's offering. That made Cain angry.

God said to Cain, "Why are you angry? I will be

happy if you do right. But I must punish you if you keep doing wrong."

Cain did not listen to God. Cain kept doing wrong. One day Cain said to Abel, "Let's go to the field." Abel went with Cain. Then Cain killed Abel.

God said to Cain, "Where is your brother?"

"How should I know?" Cain said to God.

"I know that you killed your brother," God said. "Now you must go away from home. You will have to move from place to place."

Cain was sad. And God was sad too.

To Remember

God, create a pure heart in me.
Give me a new spirit that is faithful to you.

Psalm 51:10

God Cares for Noah

God was sad and disappointed because the people he had made were not doing what was right. People were so evil all the time that God decided to flood the earth with water to destroy all the people who were not good.

But Noah pleased God. Noah lived the way God wanted him to live.

God told Noah about his plan to destroy people with

a big flood because they were so evil. But God cared about Noah's safety. He told Noah how to be safe through the flood.

God said to Noah, "I am going to put an end to all people. Make yourself an ark of wood." (An ark is a big boat.)

God told Noah to build the ark 450 feet long, 75 feet wide, and 45 feet high. God said to put a roof on it and build three levels inside. The ark needed to be big and strong and safe for Noah, his family, and the animals God wanted Noah to take with him on the ark.

Then God said, "You and your sons and your wife and your sons' wives will go into the ark. And you will bring

two of all the animals into the ark with you to keep them safe through the flood I will send. Take every kind of food you and your family and all the animals will need so all of you can eat while you're on the ark."

Noah and his three sons built the ark just the way God told them to. It took a long time for Noah and his sons to finish the ark.

Noah put food into the ark and brought his family onto the gigantic boat.

God sent two of all the animals to Noah, and he brought them onto the huge boat. There were two cows and two mice. God sent two tigers and a pair of turtles. Pairs of deer, dogs, and ostriches came because God made it happen. Two of every kind of animal came and went up into the ark.

Everything was ready. Then God shut the doors to the ark.

God sent the rain, just as he said he would. So much rain fell that even the tallest mountains were covered with water. Everything on the earth died, but God kept Noah, his family, and the animals safe just as he said he would.

To Remember

Noah did everything exactly as God commanded him.   Genesis 6:22

Did You Know?

It took Noah 120 years to build the ark. No one had ever seen an ark before, so his neighbors thought he was crazy. The whole time Noah was building the ark, everyone laughed at him. They didn't believe he was obeying God. Always do what God says no matter what your friends say or do to make fun of you. You will always be right if you obey God.

Genesis 8–9

Noah Shows Love to God

God stopped the rain after forty days. The earth was covered with water—even the tallest mountains were under water. Noah and his family and the animals were safe in the ark, floating on the water.

Slowly the flood waters dried up, and more and more

land appeared. Finally the ark landed on a mountain. Soon Noah opened a window of the ark so the sun could shine in. Before long, Noah could see that the ground was dry.

When the earth dried, God said, "Noah, come out of the ark with your family. Let out all the animals, too."

Noah obeyed. He opened the doors, and he and his family left the ark. The animals followed him.

When Noah stepped on dry ground, he wanted to show love for God by thanking him. Right away, Noah built an altar for God. Then Noah worshipped God and prayed.

God was pleased that Noah showed his love by obeying and thanking him. Then God made a promise. He said, "I will never again cover the whole earth with water."

God put a sign of his promise in the sky. Sometimes, after a rain, you can see it. A rainbow reminds us of God's promise to never again flood the whole earth.

To Remember

So God said to Noah, "The rainbow is the sign of my covenant. I have made my covenant between me and all life on earth."
Genesis 9:17

Prayer Point

When Noah and his family and all the animals got safely off the ark, Noah quickly thanked God by building an altar. God loves it when we show him we love him. How do you show your thanks and love to God?

God Calls Abraham

O ne day God told Abraham about his plan. He said, "Abraham, I have planned for you to move to a new country. When you are in your new land, I will bless you so things will go well for you."

Abraham listened to God's plan for him. He clearly heard and understood what God wanted him to do. Abraham probably knew that following God's plan might not be easy. After all, he would have to leave his relatives and his home. But Abraham would follow God's plan because he trusted God. He knew that following God's plan was the most important thing he could do.

Abraham knew how to obey God's plan. His first step was to tell his family they were moving and to start packing everything they owned. He told his wife, Sarah, and his nephew, Lot, who lived with them, about God's plan. Abraham explained that God would give them directions to their new home. Sarah and Lot were ready to follow God's plan for Abraham. They helped get ready to move. Sarah packed the water jugs and dishes. Abraham and Lot took down the tents. Abraham, Sarah, and Lot loaded their things onto camels. The people who worked for

Abraham gathered all the animals together.

The day came when Abraham was ready to start traveling to his new land. Abraham didn't know how to get there, but he trusted God to show the way. God was faithful; he showed Abraham the way to go.

Abraham, Sarah, Lot, their workers, and all their animals walked to the new country God gave to Abraham. Walking was how they traveled. God guided them all the way. He kept them safe and provided food and water as they traveled.

After traveling many days, they arrived in the country God was giving to Abraham. They could tell by looking at the land that God's plan was very good. They set up their tents, and Abraham built an altar to worship God. He thanked God for leading them safely to their new home.

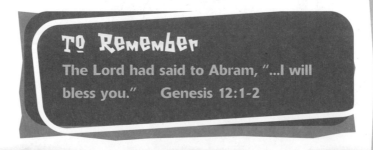

TO REMEMBER

The Lord had said to Abram, "...I will bless you."   Genesis 12:1-2

Abraham and Lot Part Company

Abraham lived in the land God gave him. God helped him have many sheep and cows.

His nephew Lot had many animals too. Servants helped take care of the animals.

Soon there were too many animals in one place. Abraham's servants wanted grassy land and water for Abraham's animals.

Lot's servants wanted grassy land and water for Lot's animals.

The servants didn't want to share. So they began to argue.

Abraham said to Lot, "We must not argue. Our servants must not argue. I will share my land with you. You pick the land you want. I will take the other part."

Lot picked the flat, grassy land. So Abraham stayed in his tent in the hills. Lot moved his tent to better land. But

Abraham was not angry.

God was pleased with Abraham. God said, "I will take care of you. I will take care of your family. I will give you all the land that you can see from here."

To Remember

If possible, live in peace with everyone. Do that as much as you can.

Romans 12:18

Lot Leaves Town

ot and his family were in danger. The people of
Sodom, where Lot lived, were very wicked and sinful.
God decided to destroy the city!

Two angels visited Lot and warned him.

But Lot wasn't in a hurry to leave to leave. The angels
said, "Hurry up! Take your wife and your two daughters.
Get out!"

"Run to the mountains," they said. "And don't look
back."

Just as they left, God rained fire down on the city. The
city and the entire valley it was in were destroyed.

While they ran, Lot's wife looked back, even though
she'd been warned not to. When she looked, she turned
into a pillar of salt.

Lot and his daughters did not look back, but ran. They
found safety in the mountains. God was merciful to them.

TO Remember

The Lord is the one who keeps you safe. So let the Most High God be like a home to you.

Psalm 91:9

God Keeps His Promise to Abraham

One night God told Abraham that he would take care of Abraham and his family and make him successful in his new land.

God said, "I will give you a son." Then God told Abraham to go outside to look at the sky. God said, "Count the stars, if you can. You will have so many grandchildren and great-grandchildren and people who will say they are part of your family, they will be as many as the stars in the sky!"

Abraham wanted a family, and God promised a very big family. Abraham believed God's promise. He completely trusted God to give him a son.

More years went by, and Abraham and Sarah still didn't have a child. Through these years of waiting, Abraham and Sarah never forgot God's promise.

God kept his promise to Abraham. Abraham and Sarah had a baby boy. They named him Isaac. The name "Isaac" means "laughter."

After Isaac was born, Sarah laughed out loud because she was so happy to have a child. She said, "God has made me happy, and everyone who hears how God has kept his promise will rejoice and be happy with me."

TO REMEMBER

The Lord took Abram outside and said, "Look up at the sky. Count the stars, if you can." Then he said to him, "That is how many children you will have." Abram believed the Lord.

Genesis 15:5-6

What Was That?

God's special promise to Abraham is called a covenant. Sarah and Abraham had to wait for years for God to keep his promise to them. God always keeps his promises. Do you always keep your promises?

God Tests Abraham

God had big plans for Abraham.

God had called Abraham to move to a new land. God had given Abraham a special son named Isaac. God had given Abraham great promises about Isaac.

Abraham was a very old man when Isaac was born. He must have felt very happy to finally have Isaac! Abraham and Sarah loved Isaac very much and took good care of him.

But a day came when God told Abraham to do a hard thing.

God told Abraham to give Isaac as a sacrifice. That meant that Isaac would have to die!

If Isaac died, Abraham would be very sad. If Isaac died, how could God's promises come true?

But Abraham trusted God. He believed God had a plan. Abraham chose to obey God. It was very hard.

Abraham began to get things ready.

Isaac asked Abraham, "I know you want to make a sacrifice to the Lord. But where is the lamb?"

Abraham said, "The Lord will give us what we need."

Abraham was ready to give Isaac as a sacrifice to God.

Suddenly, a voice called to Abraham. "Stop! Don't hurt Isaac!"

The voice was God's. God had only wanted to test that Abraham loved and trusted him more than anything. Abraham was happy. He saw a ram nearby. He sacrificed it instead of Isaac.

God blessed Abraham and gave him a big family. And Abraham was glad he had trusted God.

To Remember

Trust in the Lord forever. The Lord is the Rock. The Lord will keep us safe forever.   Isaiah 26:4

Isaac Gets a Wife

I saac was not little anymore. He was a grown-up man. Abraham loved his grown-up son Isaac. He wanted Isaac to have a wife who loved God.

Abraham asked his best servant to help. "Go to the land where I lived before. Find a good wife for Isaac there. God will help you."

The servant traveled many days by camel. When he came to a city where Abraham once lived, he stopped to

rest by a well.

The servant prayed to God. "Help me find a wife for Isaac. I'll ask a young girl for water. If she gives the camels water too, she will be right for Isaac."

A girl came to the well. She filled her pitcher with water. The servant went over to the girl.

"May I have a drink?" he asked.

"Yes," she answered. "I'll give your camels a drink too."

"Tell me your name," the servant said.

"I am Rebekah. Please stay with my family."

The servant went home with Rebekah. He told Rebekah's family why he had come. They said she could marry Isaac.

The next day Rebekah went with the servant. They traveled back to Isaac's home.

Isaac ran to meet Rebekah. They loved each other at once.

Rebekah became Isaac's wife.

To Remember

Godly people cry out, and the Lord hears them. He saves them from all of their troubles.

Psalm 34:17

Isaac's Neighbors Pick a Fight

God continued to bless Isaac. That means that God made things go very well for Isaac. Isaac realized God's blessing each harvest time when he always gathered more crops from his land than his neighbors. Isaac's sheep always had more lambs too. He had many wells that always had plenty of good water. All of these good

things were caused by God's blessing on Isaac.

Most things were going great for Isaac. He was happy, healthy, and becoming rich from farming. But his neighbors didn't like him because he had it so good. They were jealous of Isaac's success.

Isaac's neighbors thought of a way to hurt Isaac. They shoveled dirt and rocks into his wells so they were full of earth and not water. They hoped that if Isaac didn't have any water, he might leave.

When Isaac found out what happened, his neighbors said, "Go away from us. You are too successful, and we don't like you." His neighbors weren't very nice!

Isaac could have dug the dirt out of his wells and fought with his neighbors to punish them. Isaac probably

could have made his neighbors move away. But Isaac wanted to get along. He didn't want to be mean and fight with his neighbors. But Isaac still wanted to protect himself. He wasn't going to just stand around and let people be mean to

him. Isaac decided to do the only thing he could to get along. He moved away.

Isaac moved his whole family, his workers, and his animals to the place his father, Abraham, had lived many years ago. When they arrived, Isaac told his workers to dig out the wells Abraham had dug. People who didn't like Abraham had filled them in when Abraham died.

Soon Isaac had plenty of water for his animals. Isaac's new neighbors saw what he'd done. They said, "Hey, you're taking our water! You can't do that."

Again, Isaac

didn't argue or fight back. Instead, he had his workers dig a new well in a different place. But again the neighbors argued that Isaac was taking their water.

Once again, Isaac moved his family, workers, and animals to another place. This time Isaac had his workers dig a well to get water from deep in the ground. No one complained or argued with Isaac. Isaac was showing that he cared for others by getting along.

To Remember

Turn away from evil, and do good. Look for peace, and go after it.   Psalm 34:14

53

Jacob Tricks His Father

Esau and Jacob were twin brothers. Esau was born a few minutes before Jacob.

One day Esau went hunting. Jacob made some soup. Esau came home and said, "Give me some soup right away," he said.

Jacob said, "I'll give you some soup if you let me be the leader of the family instead of you."

Esau didn't think about how special it would be to be the head of the family. "You may be the leader," he said.

Isaac was Jacob and Esau's father. Many years went by, and Isaac grew very old. "I will bless you, Esau," said Isaac. "But bring me some deer meat first."

Esau went hunting, but Jacob's mother fixed some goat meat. Then she put goatskins on his arms so he would feel hairy like Esau. This way Jacob could be blessed.

Jacob knew his father could not see. So Jacob said to his father, "I am Esau, and I want you to bless me now."

Isaac felt Jacob's arms. He thought it was Esau. So Isaac blessed Jacob. He prayed, "May God give you many things. You will be the leader of this family."

Then Esau came home with deer meat. He asked his father to bless him.

"Who are you?" asked Isaac.

"I am your son, Esau."

Jacob saw that Esau was very angry. So Jacob went far away from his family for a very long time.

TO REMEMBER

Each of you must get rid of your lying. Speak the truth to your neighbor.   Ephesians 4:25

Jacob and Esau Forgive

Esau got mad when he found out about Jacob's mean trick. Esau didn't want to get along with Jacob; he wanted to get back at Jacob. Esau planned to kill Jacob!

Rebekah told Jacob about Esau's plan and told Jacob to go far away from home.

Jacob stayed away from home a long time. He missed home, but he wasn't going back yet. Jacob was afraid that Esau was still angry.

Years went by. Jacob married and started his own family. Esau also began his family back at home.

After many more years, Jacob decided to go back home. He packed up his big family and all his animals and set out on the journey.

Jacob didn't know if Esau was still angry, so he sent some messengers to visit Esau to find out.

Jacob said, "Take these animals to Esau as a gift from

me. Tell Esau, 'I am on my way to see you.'" Jacob hoped the gifts would help Esau be ready to forgive.

Jacob finally came close enough to see Esau. He walked slowly toward Esau and bowed down before him. Jacob wasn't playing any tricks now! But Esau ran to hug his brother and kiss him!

Jacob cried because he was so glad to see Esau. Esau cried too.

Jacob and Esau didn't do any more mean things to each other. They forgave each other and got along.

To Remember

A person must do what is right. He must be honest and tell the truth.

Isaiah 33:15

Joseph's Brothers Tell a Lie

Joseph had ten older brothers. One day Joseph's father gave him a new coat. The brothers saw the beautiful coat. They were jealous.

One night Joseph had a dream. He dreamed he had a bundle of grain. His bundle of grain stood up, and his brothers' bundles bowed down to it.

Joseph had another dream. The sun and moon and

eleven stars bowed down to him in that dream.

Joseph told his brothers about the dreams. The angry brothers said, "Do you think you'll be our king?"

Some time later, the older brothers took their sheep to the hills. After a few weeks, Joseph's father called him. "Go see how your brothers are," he said.

Joseph put on his coat and went to find his brothers.

The angry brothers saw him coming. They took Joseph's coat. They threw him into a deep, dry well.

Soon a group of men came by on camels. They were going to another country.

One brother said, "Let's sell Joseph."

The brothers took Joseph's coat. They put goat's blood on it. When they showed it to their father, he thought an animal killed Joseph. That's what the brothers wanted him to think.

Joseph was still alive. But he was a slave. The men on camels took him away. He could not go back home again.

To Remember

The fruit the Holy Spirit produces is love, joy and peace. It is being patient, kind and good. It is being faithful and gentle and having control of oneself.   Galatians 5:22-23

Joseph Helps Pharaoh

The king had put Joseph in prison. Joseph had not been bad. But somebody told a lie about him. That wasn't fair. But Joseph honored God anyway.

Joseph was a good helper in prison. Soon he had an important job. He helped watch the other men. Joseph was kind and listened to the men.

Two men in prison had dreams. God let Joseph know what the dreams meant. Joseph told the men what would happen.

And Joseph was right!

Two years went by. Then Pharaoh had a dream one day. He asked his helpers, "Who can tell me what my dream means?"

One helper of Pharaoh's had been in prison. Joseph had told the man about his dream. Now he remembered Joseph. "Joseph can help you," he told Pharaoh.

Pharaoh sent for Joseph. This was the pharaoh who had put Joseph in prison. Joseph could have been mad. But he honored God. He decided to help Pharaoh.

Pharaoh said, "Joseph, this was my dream. I saw seven fat cows eating grass. Seven thin cows ate the fat ones.

Then I saw seven heads of good grain. The grain was on a stalk. Seven thin heads of grain ate up the good grain."

God let Joseph know what the dream meant.

Joseph told Pharaoh about it. "You will have food in Egypt for seven good years. Then for seven bad years, food will not grow. Save food for the bad years."

Pharaoh asked Joseph to be his helper. Only Pharaoh was more important than Joseph!

And Joseph kept honoring God.

To Remember

I praised the Most High God. I gave honor and glory to the One who lives forever.

Daniel 4:34

What Was That?

Joseph was a great-grandson of Abraham. Joseph's father, Jacob, loved Joseph more than any of his other children. Joseph's brothers hated him, but God loved him. The brothers sold Joseph into slavery, even though he had done nothing wrong. Because Joseph honored God instead of becoming angry, God was able to use Joseph in a mighty way.

Joseph Forgives His Brothers

After he told Pharaoh what his dream meant, Joseph's job was to help people gather and store food for the years when none would grow. He and his helpers filled many barns with enough grain to feed the people.

When the seven years of extra food were finished, the seven bad years began. People couldn't grow their own food because it didn't rain for a long time. People came from all over Egypt, and even faraway countries, to buy food from Joseph. Joseph had an important job.

Joseph's brothers and father didn't know what happened to Joseph in Egypt. Joseph wasn't able to write a letter home, and Joseph's family never came to find him. They didn't even know if he was still alive!

Then Joseph's father and brothers ran out of food. And they knew the only place to get it was in Egypt. So that's where the brothers went. But they didn't know they would buy it from Joseph!

When the brothers came to ask for food, Joseph recognized them, but they didn't recognize Joseph.

Joseph finally said, "I'm Joseph, your brother who you sold to be a slave in Egypt."

The brothers thought they

were in big trouble! They were very afraid Joseph would punish them for what they had done to him long ago. They worried that Joseph might throw them in jail. Or maybe Joseph would sell them as slaves to get even.

Joseph hadn't forgotten what his brothers did to him.

Joseph knew he could be mean to get even with his brothers. He also knew that he could forgive them.

Joseph hugged each of his brothers to let them know he forgave them. Then Joseph provided food and everything his family needed. He told them to move to Egypt so they could be together again. Joseph's brothers were thankful that Joseph forgave them, and as soon as they could, they got their father and brought the whole family to Egypt to live with Joseph.

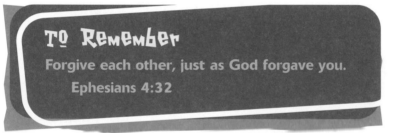

To Remember

Forgive each other, just as God forgave you.
Ephesians 4:32

Did You Know?

God always knows what will happen in the future. He is never surprised or wondering what will happen. Because Joseph was obedient to God, the big plans God had for Joseph came true. And, no matter how young you are now, God has big plans for you!

God Protects Baby Moses

Many years after Joseph died, a new pharaoh forgot all the good things Joseph had done for the people of Egypt.

Pharaoh said, "These Hebrew families are too big! I should have all the Hebrew baby boys killed so they can't make their own army and take over my kingdom!"

The Hebrew families with baby boys were sad!

One baby's mother decided to protect her baby boy. She made a basket that would float and put her baby in the basket boat. Then the mother hid the basket in the tall grass growing in the Nile River.

Miriam, the baby's big sister, watched the basket boat from a distance. Miriam knew God wanted her to care for her baby brother.

Soon Pharaoh's daughter came to the river.

She found the basket and looked inside. "This must be one of the Hebrew children," the princess said.

Miriam knew that the princess liked her brother. Miriam went up and asked, "Shall I get a Hebrew woman to help you with the baby?"

The princess said yes, so Miriam ran home and brought her mother to the princess.

The princess said to the mother, "Take good care of this baby for me. When he is no longer a baby, bring him to the palace and I will raise him like my son."

After he grew to be a young boy, his mother took him to the palace and he became the princess's son. The princess named the boy Moses because she found him in the water.

To Remember

The Lord will keep you from every kind of harm. He will watch over your life.   Psalm 121:7

Moses Sees a Burning Bush

When Moses grew up, he did not live with his people. They worked as slaves in Egypt.

Moses took care of sheep in the desert. One day Moses was with his sheep. Suddenly, he saw a bush that was on fire. But the bush did not burn up!

Then a voice came from the bush. "Moses, Moses!"

Moses knew God was talking to him from the burning bush. "I am here," Moses said.

"Take off your shoes, Moses. This is special ground," said God. "I am your God, Moses. I have seen the pain of my people. Go back to Egypt and tell Pharaoh to let the Israelite people go. I have a new land for them."

"But how can I make Pharaoh let the people go?" Moses asked God.

"I will be with you to help."

Moses was afraid. He asked, "What shall I tell them?"

God answered, "Tell them I sent you."

Moses was still afraid to do what God asked. "Send someone else," said Moses. "I don't talk very well."

God did not like what Moses said. "I made your mouth, Moses. I will help you talk to the people.

I am sending your brother, Aaron, to help you."

So Moses and Aaron went to Egypt. Moses was glad he would have Aaron to help him do what God wanted.

To Remember

My grace is all you need. My power is strongest when you are weak.   2 Corinthians 12:9

Moses and Aaron Talk to Pharaoh

After Moses saw the burning bush, he went back to Egypt to talk to Pharaoh. Moses carried the staff that God had given him.

His brother, Aaron, helped Moses talk to Pharaoh. They told Pharaoh, "You must let God's people go."

But Pharaoh said no. He did not know Israel's God.

God performed many miracles to convince Pharaoh to let God's people leave Egypt.

God sent hopping frogs that jumped into people's beds and ovens.

But Pharaoh said no.

God sent buzzing flies that flew into people's houses and even covered the ground. He sent even more disasters, called plagues, that hurt the Egyptian people.

But Pharaoh said no.

God sent pounding hail that destroyed the Egyptians' crops.

Still Pharaoh said no.

So God sent grasshoppers that ate every growing plant.

But Pharaoh still said no. Even after God sent a deep darkness that covered the land, Pharaoh still said no.

There was one more terrible plague that would come. Each Egyptian family would lose their firstborn son. And after that, Pharaoh would tell Moses and Aaron to take God's people and leave Egypt.

God had told Moses that this time Pharaoh would say yes, and Moses had told the people. So they packed their things and got ready to go!

To Remember

Obey the commands of the Lord your God.
Deuteronomy 8:6

What Was That?

God's people were called Hebrews. The Hebrews had been in slavery in Egypt for more than four hundred years, but God wanted them to be free. God sent ten plagues on Egypt to free his people. All the plagues happened to the Egyptian people, but none of the plagues happened to the Hebrews. A festival called Passover is the celebration of the time when God caused the plagues to "pass over" the Hebrews and set them free.

God's People Obey

God had told Moses he would free the Israelites. They would no longer be slaves in Egypt. He would take them to a new land that had everything they needed.

God gave Moses directions for the people. The Israelite fathers marked their doors with the blood of a lamb. When God saw the lamb's blood, he passed over those homes, and they were safe.

The Israelites also fixed a special meal. They ate lamb and flatbread. They ate in a hurry so they could leave Egypt quickly.

Everything happened just as God had told them it would.

The Egyptian families did not mark their doors with lamb's blood. And in those houses, the families lost their firstborn sons. Pharaoh lost his firstborn son too.

When this happened, Pharaoh became afraid and

angry. He told Moses, "Go! You and the Israelites must leave." He finally told them they could leave Egypt.

In fact, the Egyptian people wanted God's people to leave right away. God made the Egyptians be generous to his people. They gave the Israelites whatever they asked for—gold, silver, and clothes. The Egyptians begged the Israelites to hurry away.

So the people picked up all their treasures and anything else they could carry and began their long journey to the land God had promised them.

God had given his people a way to be saved.

To Remember

All of the people of Israel did just what the Lord had commanded Moses and Aaron.

Exodus 12:50

Moses Parts the Red Sea

After they left Egypt, the Israelites traveled for several days. They camped between some mountains with the sea in front of them. There they waited for God to lead them on.

Back in Egypt, Pharaoh changed his mind and shouted, "What have I done? I want those slaves back. Let's go get them!" He called his army together. Pharaoh and his army went in their chariots to bring the Israelites back to Egypt.

When the Israelites looked up and saw Pharaoh and his army coming after them, they were terrified! They cried out to the Lord, "Help us, God!"

Then they complained to Moses. They said, "Why did you bring us out here in the desert to die? We wish we had stayed in Egypt."

Moses told the people, "Don't be afraid. Stand firm. God will help you! Just watch as God rescues you!"

God told Moses to raise up the stick he was carrying and stretch out his hands over the sea.

God told Moses to hold his shepherd's staff over the water. Suddenly God made a strong wind blow the sea back on two sides. The sea rose up into two high walls of water with a path between. Now the people could walk through the sea on the path of dry ground God had made for them.

As the Israelites walked safely through the sea on dry ground, Pharaoh's army began to follow them. Just as God's people reached the other side, Moses again lifted up his hand over the sea. This time God stopped the wind. The water walls came crashing over Pharaoh's army. All of Pharaoh's army was drowned, but all of God's people were safe.

When they saw how God had saved them from the Egyptians, they trusted God and knew they could follow Moses as their leader.

To Remember

Because your love is faithful, you will lead the people you have set free.
Exodus 15:13

God Gives Water to His People

Moses and the Israelite people were still traveling through a desert. They were on their long trip with all of their belongings and animals. They were walking from Egypt to the land God promised to give them.

To feed the people, God sent quail, which are small, wild birds that taste like chicken, and manna, which is God's special bread that tasted like flakes with honey. God provided food for every day.

At one of the places the people camped they couldn't find water. There were no lakes or streams anywhere around. The desert was hot and dry. They were unhappy and becoming angry. They needed water, and they wanted it now!

The people should have trusted God to give them water, but they didn't. Instead, they complained to Moses as if it were his fault that they couldn't find water.

They yelled, "Give us water to drink! Did you bring us out here in the desert to die of thirst?"

Moses knew he didn't have any water. But he also knew God could give them water.

Moses asked God, "What should I do with these people?"

God would take care of his people. God told Moses to lead some of the older men to a certain large rock. God told Moses to hit the rock with his staff. (A staff is like a walking stick.) God said he would make water flow out of the rock for the people to drink.

Moses obeyed by leading the men to find the rock that God told them about.

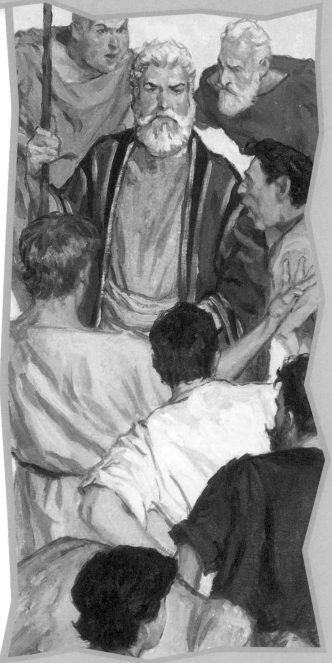

Whack! Moses hit the rock with his staff. *Whoosh!* God made water gush out of the rock. Moses and the other men knew God had done a miracle to make water come from the rock. They saw how God was taking care of them by giving them water.

Moses called the people to come and drink. Everyone was happy, and they weren't thirsty anymore because God gave them water.

God taught the people to trust him to take care of them.

To Remember

He [God] turned the rock into a pool. He turned the hard rock into springs of water.

Psalm 115:8

Prayer Pointer

Do you know that God hears us when we praise him? And he hears us when we complain, too. God heard the Hebrews when they complained about having no water. But no matter what we do, he still loves us. Thank you, God, for always loving me, and for forgiving me when I complain.

Moses Listens to Good Advice

J ethro, Moses' father-in-law, came to visit Moses at the Israelite camp. Jethro asked, "What will you do today, Moses?"

Moses said, "I will listen to people who cannot solve their problems. I'll explain God's rules so they know what God wants them to do. You may watch me."

So many people wanted Moses to listen to their problems that they had to wait their turn. The people were already unhappy with each other because they had arguments to settle. And they didn't enjoy standing in the hot sun all day waiting for a turn to let Moses settle their little fights.

At the end of the long day, Jethro asked Moses why he was trying to listen to so many people.

"Because I am the only one they can ask about God's laws," said Moses.

Jethro said, "You need some help! Let me help you learn a better way. Choose some good helpers. Let them listen to the people and help them with the easier things.

When something hard comes up, let your helpers bring the problem to you."

The helpers Moses picked taught the people about God's laws. They took the hard problems to Moses.

Now Moses had time to help the people who really needed him, and everyone got the anwers they needed.

To Remember

My son, listen to your father's advice. Don't turn away from your mother's teaching.

Proverbs 1:8

Aaron Builds a Golden Calf

The Israelites camped near Mount Sinai. Moses went up the mountain, and God talked to him for a long time. God made promises to his people and also gave Moses rules for the people to follow—including the Ten Commandments, which God wrote on flat stones.

Moses stayed up on the mountain for many days. The people forgot about him and begged Aaron to make a god for them.

Aaron made a statue of a calf out of jewelry the people brought to him. He told the people, "Here is your god who brought you up out of Egypt."

The next day, the people had a party for the calf statue! They forgot all about the great things God had done .

God saw what the people were doing. He was so angry! He told Moses to go down the mountain.

Moses was angry too! He was so angry he threw down the flat stones with God's rules on them, and they smashed into a million pieces! He invited the people who were on the Lord's side to join him. Then Moses asked God to forgive the people. God hated the idol worship, but he forgave them and continued leading them.

T̲O Remember

You [God] stopped being angry with them. You turned your burning anger away from them.

Psalm 85:3

What Was That?

When the Hebrews crossed the desert, some people worshipped a golden calf. That made God angry. He punished those bad people, but he forgave those who asked for forgiveness. Remember, God loves you and will forgive you when you sin. Never stay away from God because you think he won't forgive you.

93

God Gives the Ten Commandments

After the people told God they were sorry for worshipping the golden calf, Moses went back up the mountain to get God's rules again.

God again wrote some rules, the Ten Commandments, for all his people to obey. These rules would help us know how to live so we would please God. And God promised that if we followed his rules, we would be happy and things would go well for us. The rules would also help us know how to get along with each other.

God's first rule is "Love God." God wants us to love him more than anyone or anything. God is most important. Nothing matters more than God.

Another rule God gave is "Worship God." God gave us this rule to have us save one day each week just for him.

Another rule God gave is "Honor your father and mother." This means treat your parents with respect. God wants us to listen to and obey our parents and to be polite when we talk to them.

God also said, "Do not steal." It's wrong to take things that belong to others if we don't have their permission. Not stealing things pleases God and helps us get along with others.

One of the last rules God gave us says, "Do not lie." This means God wants us to be honest and tell the truth. Even when we think we might get in trouble, God still wants us to be honest.

Love God, worship God, honor your father and mother, do not steal, and do not lie—these are five of the rules God gave us.

To Remember

Honor your father and mother.   Exodus 20:12

God's People Give Their Talents

G od told Moses to have the Israelites build a special tent called the holy tent. It would be a place to worship God.

"We need help to build the tabernacle," Moses told the Israelites. "If you like, you may bring a gift. You may give things you have, or you may give your talents. Let's give from our hearts."

Many people brought their gifts. They brought gold, silver, and jewels. They brought cloth, wood, and special oils.

Other people gave their talents. Two men who could

make things also knew how to teach. So they taught others how to make useful things.

Some workers made things from gold, silver, and bronze. Other workers carved beautiful patterns into wood or made cloth and sewed patterns into it.

The people brought gifts every day. Finally, Moses said, "You have given a lot. We have enough."

The people had happily given their gifts and talents to build God's holy tent.

To Remember

You should each give what you have decided in your heart to give.   2 Corinthians 9:7

The Walls of Jericho Fall

After Moses died, God chose Joshua as Israel's new leader. Joshua told the people to prepare to enter the Promised Land. God dried up the Jordan River so everyone could get across and enter the land.

The people in Jericho saw the Israelites crossing the river, and they were afraid! They closed up their city and wouldn't let the Israelites in.

Joshua knew God wanted him to capture Jericho, but its walls were tall and thick. God said to Joshua, "I have

handed Jericho over to you." Then he told Joshua how to win the battle.

Joshua followed God's words exactly.

The fighting men and the priests walked around the city walls one time. And even though they were carrying swords and spears and looked tough, they never tried to fight, and they never said a word. When they finished walking around the city, they went back to their camp.

The next day they did the same thing. In fact, they silently walked one time around the city six days in a row.

On the seventh day, they marched around the city seven times instead of one. And on the seventh time, the priests blew a long blast on their trumpets. Then Joshua

told the fighting men, "Shout! The Lord has given you the city!"

So the men shouted with all their might! And at the sound, the tall, thick walls of Jericho fell flat!

The people obeyed God, and God kept his promise. The Israelites captured the city.

T̪o̪ Remember

"Don't be afraid. Don't lose hope. Be strong and brave."   Joshua 10:25

Did Y̪o̪u K̈n̈o̪w?

Jericho was the world's first city! Did you know that in Bible times cities were built inside high, thick walls for protection from enemies? If the wall around Jericho were still standing today, it would take three months to bulldoze it down!

God Chooses Gideon

After the Israelites were settled in the land God had promised them, they once again forgot all the good things he had done for them. They didn't worship or thank God. They just pretended he wasn't there and went about their business.

God was very angry. He let the Midianites attack Israel. They stole all the Israelites' food and animals.

So the people of Israel cried out to God. They wanted God to fight their enemies.

God heard them, and even though they hadn't thanked him or worshipped him, he still loved them.

A man named Gideon was doing farmwork in a hidden place so the Midianites would not take his grain. God sent an angel to Gideon. "Brave soldier, God is with you," the angel said.

"If God is with us, why are we in trouble?" Gideon asked.

"The Lord is sending you to help your people," the angel said.

"Me?" Gideon said. "But I'm the youngest in my poor family. Nobody cares what I do or say."

He was afraid of the Midianites.

"The Lord will be with you," the angel said.

Gideon wanted a sign that God would help him. He placed a sheepskin on the ground. He asked God, "If you really are going to help me, please make dew appear on the sheepskin. But keep the ground dry. Then I will know that you will help me."

The next day, there was dew on the skin. In fact, it was sopping wet! When Gideon wrung it out, the water filled a bowl! But the ground was dry.

Gideon wanted another sign. He said, "Make dew appear on the ground. But make the sheepskin dry."

God again did what Gideon asked.

Now Gideon was ready. He would do what God wanted him to do. God would help Gideon rescue his people from the Midianites.

To Remember

The Lord helps me. I will not be afraid.

Hebrews 13:6

Gideon Wins the Battle

God had chosen Gideon to lead his people. He would lead the army against the Midianites. But God had a special way to do this. God wanted to win the battle for his people.

Gideon gathered the soldiers. God said, "You have too many men. Send home the ones who are scared."

Many men left.

Then God said, "Gideon, there are still too many soldiers. Tell the men to drink from the river. Count the men who use their hands to scoop up the water. Only these men will fight." Gideon sent all the others home. Only three hundred soldiers were left. That was not enough to win a battle.

But Gideon trusted God.

God told Gideon to fight the Midianites at night. Each man took a trumpet. Each man took a torch of fire hidden inside a jar. While the Midianites were sleeping, the men blew their trumpets. They broke their jars and let the fires shine.

The Midianites woke up and thought they were surrounded by a huge army! They were afraid and ran away.

Gideon and his people were safe again. God showed that his way was the best way.

TO REMEMBER

"My thoughts are not like your thoughts. And your ways are not like my ways," announces the Lord.   Isaiah 55:8

Did You Know?

Did you know that the soldiers drank from a spring called Spring of Harod? This spring is full of leeches. So only the soldiers who drank from their hands knew if they were swallowing leeches!

Hannah Asks God for a Child

Hannah was a woman who loved God. But Hannah was very sad because she did not have any children.

One day she went to God's house.

Hannah told God how sad she was. She prayed and prayed. "Dear God, please give me a little boy. If you do, I will raise him to love you, and he will be your helper always."

Hannah kept praying for a long time.

A priest named Eli saw her. At first he was worried about her, but then he realized that she was very sad. Eli told her, "Don't be sad. May God give you what you prayed for."

Hannah didn't feel sad anymore. She went back home. Soon God did answer Hannah's prayer! God gave her and her husband a baby boy.

Hannah named the baby Samuel. His name meant "asked of God." How Hannah loved her baby! She fed him and made little clothes for him. She took good care of him. Hannah was thankful to God for saying yes to her prayer.

As Samuel grew bigger, Hannah remembered her promise to God. Hannah told Samuel about God's house. She told him about Eli the priest. She helped Samuel learn to love and obey God and be God's helper.

Then the time came for Samuel to be a helper at God's house. Hannah took Samuel to Eli, the priest. Hannah said to him, "Remember how I prayed for a son? Look! God gave him to me. Now I am giving him to God. My son will always be God's helper."

Then Hannah gave thanks to God for answering her prayer.

To Remember

Lord, in the morning you hear my voice. In the morning I pray to you. I wait for you in hope.
Psalm 5:3

God Chooses Saul to Be King

Samuel had led the people of Israel for many years.

One day the Israelites went to Samuel. They said, "Samuel, you are too old. We need a new leader. We want a king, like all the countries around us. Find us a king!"

Samuel went off to pray. God told him what to do: "Let them have a king if that's what they want. But tell them it's not my plan."

Samuel told the people God's words.

The people told Samuel, "We want a king anyway."

Samuel went to a young man named Saul. Samuel poured oil over his head.

Saul was now the king of the Israelites. The Israelites had not chosen God's way.

To Remember

Choose for yourselves right now whom you will serve. Joshua 24:15

Saul Disobeys God

Saul was Israel's first king. In the beginning of his reign, he followed God's ways.

When Saul had led Israel for about twenty years, God told him to fight a battle a certain way.

But Saul did it his way, and God was not pleased!

Samuel went to see Saul to tell him God was angry.

"But, Samuel, I did obey the Lord," Saul said. "I fought the enemy and I brought back animals to sacrifice to God."

But Samuel replied, "God didn't ask you to bring back animals!

116

What pleases the Lord more? Burnt offerings and sacrifices, or obeying him? It is better to obey than to offer a sacrifice."

Because of Saul's sin, God rejected him as king. When Samuel turned to leave, Saul grabbed Samuel's robe and tore it. Samuel told Saul God would tear the kingdom of Israel from Saul and give it to one who would obey God with all his heart. Later, God told Samuel to go to Bethlehem to find and anoint the next king.

God had Samuel anoint David as the next king of Israel. God knew that David would obey him with all his heart.

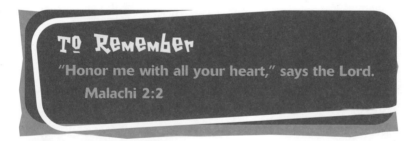

To Remember

"Honor me with all your heart," says the Lord.
   Malachi 2:2

In Ancient Times

A long time ago it was common to put oil on someone's head to anoint them. To anoint someone means that person has a special purpose in his life. Did you know that Samuel put oil on David's head to anoint him as the next king of Israel? Samuel used a special oil made from a recipe God gave Moses. The olive oil was mixed with cinnamon, cane, cassia, and myrrh.

David Fights a Giant

David's older brothers were soldiers in the Israelite army. They went to fight an enemy army.

David watched his father's sheep. He kept them safe from lions and bears.

One day David's father told him, "Take some food to your brothers."

When David found his brothers, they weren't fighting the enemy. All of the soldiers were afraid!

"What is the matter?" David asked.

"You'll see," his brothers said.

Soon an enemy soldier walked out. He was a huge giant named Goliath.

"I want a man to fight me!" he shouted to the Israelites.

But none of the soldiers moved.

David said to the soldiers, "We should not be afraid of this giant. God is on our side. He will help us."

King Saul heard about the brave

young man. He sent for David. "You are just a boy," King Saul said.

"I will fight the giant," David said. "God helped me kill a lion and a bear. I know he will help me kill this giant."

David picked up his shepherd's staff and five stones for his sling. Then he went out to meet Goliath.

The giant had a heavy sword, a long spear, and a huge

shield. Goliath laughed when he saw David.

"Why are you coming at me with sticks? Do you think I'm only a dog?" asked Goliath. "Come over here!"

David said, "You are coming to fight against me with a sword and a spear. But I'm coming against you in the name of the Lord who rules over all. He is the God of the armies of Israel. He's the one you have dared to fight against.

"This very day the Lord will hand you over to me. The Lord doesn't save by using a sword or a spear. And everyone who is here will know it. The battle belongs to the Lord."

David put a stone in his sling. He pulled back the sling and let it go. The stone flew out of the sling and hit the giant in the head.

Goliath fell down dead.

Then the Israelites chased away the enemy army. David had trusted God's great power, and God delivered him from the giant.

To Remember

Let the Lord make you strong. Depend on his mighty power.   Ephesians 6:10

David Helps Saul

David was King Saul's helper. David played the harp for Saul and led battles for Saul. God helped David win the battles.

The people of Israel loved David. They sang songs about him.

"King Saul has won many battles," they sang. "But David has won the most!"

King Saul became jealous of David. One day David was playing the harp. King Saul was feeling angry.

He threw a spear at David to kill him. But he missed.

David had to run away and hide. He hid for many years because Saul kept trying to kill him.

But David kept trusting God.

To Remember

When I'm afraid, I will trust in you. Psalm 56:3

David and Jonathan Become Friends

David was a young man who knew God loved him very much. David loved God and knew God would always take care of him.

At that time, King Saul liked David because he was so brave. Saul asked David to come live with him. So David went to live at King Saul's palace.

The king's son, Jonathan, became friends with David. Jonathan did things for David that showed he was David's friend. He made a promise to be David's friend. Jonathan took off his own coat and gave it to David. Then Jonathan gave David his sword, bow, and belt. They were very special gifts. Jonathan gave David these gifts because he loved David and wanted to be David's best friend.

David accepted Jonathan's gifts. He knew Jonathan would be his friend for a long, long time.

David did many great things to help the people of Israel. God blessed David, and King Saul grew jealous of David's success.

Once Jonathan was talking with his father, King Saul. Even though Saul was unhappy with David, Jonathan told his father why David was a good friend. He reminded his father of all the good things David had done. He asked his father not to be angry with David.

Jonathan was a best friend to David. He loved David like he loved himself.

David also knew how to be a friend. David showed his friendship by promising to always be kind to Jonathan and everyone in Jonathan's family.

Jonathan and David both knew that God

would make David the king someday. Jonathan knew David's promise would be very important for his safety and his family's safety when David became king of Israel. And David showed he was a good friend by keeping his promise for the rest of his life.

To Remember

A friend loves at all times. He is there to help when trouble comes.   Proverbs 17:17

Prayer Point

David knew that one day he would be king. He had the right skills for it, but he knew to wait for God's timing. What do you know how to do that God can use now and later? Thank you, God, that you show us how to use our special skills for you.

David Spares Saul's Life

King Saul was looking for David. The king wanted to kill him.

David tried to hide with his men. He moved from town to town. He hid in caves and in the woods. But he was never safe from King Saul.

One day King Saul found out where David was. The king and his army marched after David.

When nighttime came, the king's soldiers set up a camp. They put the king's bed in the middle. A special guard slept by the king to keep him safe.

King Saul lay down to rest. His spear and water jug

were next to him. Soon he fell fast asleep. The guard and all the soldiers fell asleep too.

Later, David came with one of his men, Abishai. They saw the king's men all sound asleep!

"Let's go closer to the king," said David. The two men walked right up to Saul.

"I will kill the king," Abishai said. "Then he will not hurt you anymore."

"No!" said David. "Saul is the king. We must not hurt the leader God chose."

David and his friend took the king's spear and water jug and went to a nearby hill.

David shouted to the king's guard, "You have not taken good care of your king. Someone could have hurt him."

King Saul woke up and heard David's voice. He saw that his spear and water jug were gone. He knew David could have killed him. "I am sorry I chased you, David," said Saul.

David said, "I could have killed you today, but I will not hurt the king God has chosen. Now may God keep me safe too."

Saul said, "May God bless you. You will do great things."

Then David went away with his men. And King Saul went home.

T̊ Rememb̊er

Hate stirs up fights. But love erases all sins by forgiving them.   Proverbs 10:12

David Dances

One day King Saul was in a battle. He and his son Jonathan both died. David cried when he heard the news.

God's people did not have a king anymore. So they came to David and asked him to be the new king. David knew God's promise had come true.

David wanted to bring the ark of God to Jerusalem to

remind the people that God was with them.

The day the ark came to Jerusalem was just like a party! All the people came out to show their joy and respect for God. They shouted and blew trumpets. David was so happy he danced in the streets in praise to God!

To Remember

Praise the Lord for the glory that belongs to him.   Psalm 29:2

SOLOMON Chooses Wisdom

When David was very old, he made his son Solomon the king of Israel. Because he was king, Solomon had to make a lot of choices about how to rule the people. Solomon wanted to be a good king by making good choices. He knew making good choices would please God.

Sometimes Solomon would look out at the people who lived in Israel. He would think about some of the decisions he had to make and what the good choices were. He worried that he might not always make good choices.

One night when Solomon was resting, God talked with him. God gave Solomon another choice to make! God said, "Ask for whatever you want me to give you."

Solomon might have asked God for all the money in the world. He could have asked to live a long time. He could have asked that he wouldn't need to fight any battles. But Solomon didn't ask for any of these.

Solomon said to God, "Make me wise, so I can rule over your people and tell the difference between right and wrong." Solomon asked God to make him wise so he could make good choices.

God was pleased with Solomon's good choice. God said, "I will give you a wise and understanding heart." God made Solomon so wise that there never has been anyone as wise as Solomon besides Jesus, and there never will be a person as wise as Solomon. He will always be known as the wisest person ever.

God was so pleased with Solomon's good choice that God said, "I will give you some things you didn't ask for." God gave Solomon great riches and honor, and he made Solomon the greatest king alive.

Solomon was happy that God gave him a wise and understanding heart. He knew that he could be a good king for the people and please God by making good choices.

To Remember

Wisdom is best. So get wisdom. No matter what it costs, get understanding.   Proverbs 4:7

Who Was That?

Solomon was King David's son. Solomon was going to be the king after David, so God asked Solomon what special gift he wanted to help him rule over Israel. Solomon asked God for wisdom. Isn't that amazing? He could have asked for money or anything else, but Solomon just wanted to be wise and pleasing to God. God has given everyone special gifts. Did you know that if you let God lead you in using those gifts, he will bless you more and more?

SOLOMON USES GOD'S WISDOM

People came to hear Solomon. Solomon was the wisest man who ever lived. He had asked God to give him wisdom. So the people wanted to hear his wise teaching.

People came to Solomon when they needed help with a problem. Solomon gave good advice.

One day two women came to Solomon. They knew that he gave good

advice, and they had a serious problem. These women lived together. Each woman had a new baby. But one of the babies died. His sad mother stole the other baby and said it was hers!

They both went to the king to solve this problem.

"Which one of you is the mother?" Solomon asked the women.

"I am!" one woman said.

"No, I am!" said the other.

King Solomon said, "Since you both claim to be the baby's mother, there is only one thing to do. Bring me a sword," the king said. "Cut the baby in two. Each of you shall have half."

"No!" cried one woman. "Please don't cut him in two. Let her have him!"

The other woman said, "Go ahead! Cut him in two!"

Then the king knew the truth. The real mother was the one who loved the baby and wanted him to live.

"Give the child to her," he said. "She is the child's mother."

God's wisdom helped Solomon know what to do. He also wrote down good advice in wise sayings called proverbs. Proverbs is a book in our Bible. Solomon wrote many proverbs about words. Our words can hurt people, Solomon wrote, and our words can help people.

Solomon wrote, "Be careful what you say. Use your words to help others."

To Remember

The mouths of those who do what is right speak wisdom. They say what is honest.
Psalm 37:30

SOLOMON Follows God's Plan for the Temple

King Solomon wanted to build a place to worship God, so he gathered together wood and stone, gold and silver, and gems.

Many people worked hard to build the temple. Solomon used only the best workers and the best supplies.

Crash! Bang! The workers cut logs. *Boom! Clank!* The workers shaped the stones. *Zip! Scrape!* The workers sewed cloth and carved decorations.

The temple had a special room. It was called the Most Holy Room. The ark of God was kept in this room. It meant God was near.

Only the high priest could enter the Most Holy Room. He would pray to God about the sins of the people. No one else could go so close to God's room. A curtain hung in front of the door to make sure no one would look in.

People brought animals to the temple to offer as sacrifices. That means they were killed on an altar. Then

God would forgive the sins of his people.

Many years passed. Jesus came to earth. He died on a cross. He was the perfect sacrifice. He offered his own life instead of animals.

When Jesus died, the curtain of the Most Holy Room was torn apart from the top to the bottom. The way to God was opened. Then Jesus went into heaven to pray for us.

Now we can go right to God if we believe in Jesus. We don't have to go through a building. We don't have to offer an animal. Jesus opened the way to God.

To Remember

Jesus gave one sacrifice for the sins of the people. He gave it once and for all time. He did it by offering himself.   Hebrews 7:27

Did You Know?

Did you know that special cedar logs were used to build the temple? Those logs came from a country called Lebanon. The logs from these cedar trees were a beautiful red color, and they smelled good too. The workers floated the logs down the rivers till they reached the place where the temple was being built. Solomon used only the best when he built the temple.

SOLOMON WORSHIPS GOD with Prayer

Solomon hired workers to build the temple. It took seven years. When the temple was finished, Solomon invited all the priests and people to come worship God at the temple.

Everyone came. They gathered in the large open area in front of the temple. It was like a grand opening. This was the first time the people could worship at the new temple.

While everyone watched, the priests brought the last piece of furniture up the steps and through the doors into the temple. The last piece was the ark of God. The priests left the ark in the temple.

When they came out of the temple, God went into his temple to be there in a special way. A cloud filled the temple to show that the glory of the Lord was there. It was as if God had moved in, yet he was also everywhere else. Everyone knew that no building could ever keep God inside.

Then Solomon knelt down in front of all the people to

pray. He wanted to pray to worship God.

Solomon prayed, "We praise you, God, for keeping your promises. We praise you that we can trust you. Thank you for your great love. And now, God, we ask you these things: Please keep your promises, please listen to each of us when we pray, and please forgive us."

When Solomon was done praying, he stood up and talked to the people. Solomon encouraged everyone to worship God by praying. He reminded them to praise God, to thank God, and to ask God to forgive them.

To Remember

I praise the Lord. He has given peace and rest to his people.   1 Kings 8:56

Elijah Sees God's Power

Ahab was a king who did not obey God or worship God. He worshipped a false god named Baal.

Elijah was a man who loved God. God made Elijah a prophet and gave him a message for King Ahab.

Elijah said to Ahab, "You have done many wicked things. So God will not let it rain in your kingdom until I say so."

King Ahab was angry. He wanted to hurt Elijah. But God kept Elijah safe. God told Elijah to hide near a brook. Even though it did not rain, Elijah had water to drink. God sent birds with food for Elijah.

After three years without rain, God sent Elijah to King Ahab again. Elijah said, "You have sinned by worshipping your false god, Baal, instead of worshipping the one true God. Tell all the people and the prophets of Baal to meet me on Mount Carmel."

When everyone was together, Elijah said, "How long will you worship Baal instead of God? Today you will find out who is the one true God! You should follow him."

Elijah told all the false prophets to build an altar and put an offering on it. Elijah also built an altar and put an offering on it.

Elijah said, "You can call to your god Baal. I will call on the name of the Lord. The one who answers by sending fire to burn up the offering—that is the true God."

The false prophets did what Elijah said. They called on Baal all morning. But no fire came to burn the offering.

Elijah said, "Shout louder! Maybe Baal can't hear you."

The false prophets called on Baal until it was nearly dark. But Baal didn't answer. No fire came down.

Elijah said to the people, "Come with me." Elijah poured water over the altar he had made. Then Elijah called on God. Elijah said, "O Lord, answer me. Show us your mighty power. Then these people will know you are the one true God."

God answered Elijah. The fire came down. It burned up the offering. It burned up the altar. It even burned up the water!

When the people saw this, they knew they had been wrong. They were sorry they had worshipped Baal. They fell down and said, "The Lord—he is God! The Lord—he is God!"

To Remember

The Lord is the great God. He is the greatest King. He rules over all of the gods.
Psalm 95:3

Elijah Hears God's Voice

On Mount Carmel God had shown King Ahab and the people that he was the real God by sending fire to burn the altar. Then God sent rain as he promised. But wicked Queen Jezebel was angry. She wanted to kill Elijah.

Elijah was afraid. He ran into the desert and sat under a tree. But God took care of Elijah.

Soon an angel came and woke him up. The angel brought food and water.

After Elijah ate, he climbed a mountain and hid in a cave. Elijah felt all alone and afraid. He thought he was the only one left who believed in God. God wanted to help Elijah feel better.

God said, "Go out and stand on the mountain. I am going to pass by."

As Elijah stood on the mountain, God sent a strong wind. The wind broke the rocks into pieces.

But the Lord wasn't in the wind.

Then God sent an earthquake. The ground shook and shook. But the Lord wasn't in the earthquake.

And then came a fire that crackled and burned. But the Lord wasn't in the fire.

Elijah was in the middle of the wind, earthquake, and fire. But Elijah wasn't hurt. God took care of him.

Then Elijah heard a whisper. It was God! God was

talking to Elijah in a whisper.

God told Elijah what to do. He said a man named Elisha would be Elijah's new helper. God told Elijah that he wasn't alone. He didn't need to be afraid.

Elijah listened to God's voice. Elijah knew God would always take care of him, and didn't feel so alone and afraid anymore.

He went down the mountain to find his new helper, Elisha.

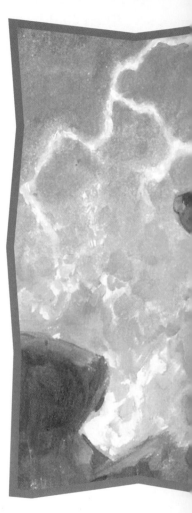

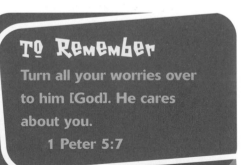

To Remember

Turn all your worries over to him [God]. He cares about you.

1 Peter 5:7

Elijah Goes to Heaven

E lijah and his new helper, Elisha, were about to leave a place called Gilgal. Elijah knew that soon God was going to take him to heaven in a strong wind. He wouldn't die, but he would go to be with God!

Elijah said to Elisha, "God told me to go to Bethel. You stay here."

Elisha was sad. His friend was going to heaven. He wanted to be with Elijah as long as he could.

"I won't leave you," said Elisha. So, they both went to Bethel.

Soon, Elijah said God wanted him to leave Bethel and go to Jericho.

"You stay here," he told Elisha. But Elisha wouldn't stay. So, they both traveled to Jericho.

God then told Elijah to go to the Jordan River.

"Stay here," Elijah said to his helper. But Elisha wanted to go with Elijah.

The two men went to the Jordan River with many others. Elijah put his coat in the water. Suddenly, the water parted. There was dry land in the middle of the river!

Elijah and Elisha walked on the dry land to the other side.

Elijah wanted to do something for his helper before he left. Elisha had done so much for him.

"What can I do for you before I go?" Elijah asked.

Elisha knew it would be hard to do the work Elijah had done. He knew he needed God's help.

He said he wanted God to be with him even more that God had been with Elijah.

"If you see me go up to heaven," Elijah said, "then God will give you what you want."

Just then, a chariot with horses appeared. It was covered with fire! As Elijah got into the chariot, the wind began to blow harder and harder. The wind picked up the fiery chariot and took it right up to heaven!

Elisha stayed with Elijah as long as he could and saw his friend leave. He knew God would be with him just as God had been with Elijah.

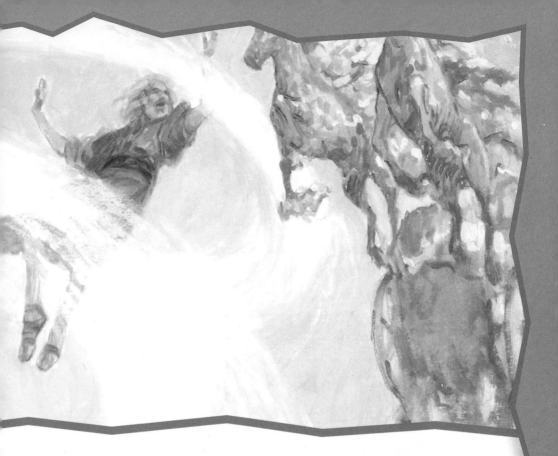

Elisha's Servant Sees Angels

The king of Aram was angry because his sneak attacks on Israel were always discovered! How was that possible? Was one of the king's own people helping the nation of Israel? Someone certainly was!

Aha! One day the king found out who was telling his secret plans to the king of Israel: Elisha, the prophet of God. So the king sent his army to the city of Dothan with one order: Capture him!

The next morning Elisha's servant woke up and went

outside. The enemy army, with horses and chariots, had surrounded the city!

The servant was terrified! He ran back into the house, and called to Elisha, "Master! What are we going to do?"

"Don't be afraid," Elisha answered. "Those who are with us are more than those who are with them."

Elisha prayed, "Lord, open my servant's eyes so he can see." Then the Lord opened the servant's eyes. He looked out at the hills. They were full of horses and chariots of

fire all around
Elisha.

At that moment,
the enemy army
came galloping
toward Elisha.

Elisha prayed
again. This time he
said, "Lord, make
the soldiers blind."
And God answered
his prayer.

Elisha said to the soldiers, "You're in the wrong place.
Follow me. I'll lead you to where you need to go."

He led them all right—right into the middle of the
camp of Israel's army!

Once the soldiers were inside, the Lord opened their
eyes when Elisha asked him to. The soldiers realized that
instead of capturing Elisha, they had been captured
themselves!

The king of Israel asked Elisha what to do with the
enemy soldiers. Elisha told him, "Feed them and send
them home."

When the soldiers finished eating, they went back
home. And those men never again attacked Israel.

TO Remember

Love your enemies. Pray for those who hurt you.   Matthew 5:44

Did You Know?

You can trust God to be there for you when you need him. Remember, God loves you and wants what is best for you. But did you know that he also loves your enemies and wants you to love them too? That's hard to do, but God will help you to love your enemies if you'll let him.

Josiah Listens to God's Word

When a king died, one of his sons would become the next king. Josiah was only eight years old when his father died. Imagine being a king when you are only eight!

Josiah knew God and loved him. Josiah knew he could be a good king if he obeyed God like King David did many years before.

Many kings of Israel weren't good leaders because they didn't love God and didn't help the people to worship and obey God. Even Josiah's father didn't worship God.

Kings who didn't love God usually didn't take care of the temple. Since Josiah's father and other kings before him didn't take care of the temple, it was falling apart. The walls and floors had cracks. Some of the stone blocks needed to be replaced. The wood doors and roof needed work. Josiah decided to fix up the temple.

Josiah told his helpers, "Pay some workers to repair the temple."

Soon workers began to fill the cracks and holes. They replaced broken stone blocks with new stone blocks. They brought wood to fix the roof and doors. The temple would be like new again.

On one of the work-days, the temple priest found something that didn't belong where it was. The priest found a scroll.

A scroll is a Bible-time book. Scrolls were made from a long piece of special paper called *papyrus* rolled around two sticks. God's Word was written on the rolled-up papyrus. This scroll was like our Bible because it had God's Word.

The temple priest read the scroll and knew he had found God's Word. He gave the scroll to King Josiah's helper. The king's helper also read the scroll and knew it was God's Word. He took the scroll to the king.

"King Josiah! Look at this scroll!" the helper said. "The priest found it in the temple!"

King Josiah listened as his helper read God's Word. The scroll told how God loved his people and wanted them to listen to him and obey his Word.

King Josiah called all the people together. He read the scroll to them. Then King Josiah made a promise to listen to God's Word and obey it. When the people heard King Josiah's promise, they also promised to listen to God's Word and obey what it taught.

TO Remember

How can a young person keep his life pure? By living in keeping with your word.

Psalm 119:9

Jehoshaphat Fights God's Way

King Jehoshaphat was a good king. He trusted God and tried to do right.

One day men brought news to the king. They said, "A big enemy army is coming! They want to fight us."

The king said, "Tell the people to come to Jerusalem. We will go to the temple area and pray. God will help us."

The people hurried to the temple. The king stood up and prayed. "Dear God, a big army is coming! We do not have enough soldiers to fight a battle. Please help us."

All the people—even the children—prayed with the king.

Then one of the priests said, "God has told me to tell you this: Do not be afraid. The battle is not yours, but God's. Go out to meet the enemy tomorrow. You will not have to fight them. God will take care of everything."

King Jehoshaphat trusted God. The king didn't know how God would answer, but he knew God would do what was best.

The next morning, King Jehoshaphat and his army marched out to meet the enemy. The king went first. Then came those who sang and played music. As they

marched, their songs praised God. Next came the soldiers.

They marched up a hill. Everyone stopped and looked down into the valley.

What a surprise was in front of them! The enemy army was there, but they had fought with one another. Now the enemy soldiers were all dead!

The king and his people had not expected this answer to their prayer. God took care of everything. They didn't have to fight at all! They were glad they trusted God to do what was best.

To Remember

God, I call out to you because you will answer me. Listen to me. Hear my prayer.   Psalm 17:6

Joash and the People Worship God with Gifts

Joash was only seven years old when he became king of Israel.

When Joash was older, he decided to fix up the temple. He saw that the temple steps, walls, and pillars were cracked. Joash knew that the temple should look good to honor God. He ordered the priest and others who were supposed to take care of the temple to repair it and make it look new again. Joash told the priest to collect the offerings the people gave to pay for fixing the temple.

The priest did not collect the offerings as he should have. So Joash put a big offering box at the entrance to the temple.

King Joash announced in Jerusalem and throughout the land, "Let all the people worship God by giving gladly to the Lord."

All the people brought their gifts and gladly put them in Joash's box. Rich people put a lot of money in the box. Others didn't have a lot of money, but they still gladly gave what they had.

When the box was full, the priests emptied it and counted the money. They kept the money safe so they could use it to pay for the temple repairs. Then they put the empty box in its place at the temple. More people came to worship God by giving gladly.

Now the temple could be repaired.

King Joash and the priest used the money the people gave for the workers and materials. The king hired men who worked with wood, stone, and metal to repair the temple.

The work went well. Soon the temple was fixed. The people came to the temple. They were glad they had worshipped God by giving their offerings.

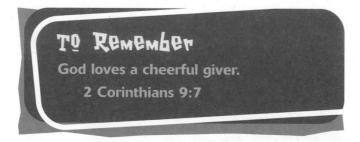

To Remember
God loves a cheerful giver.
2 Corinthians 9:7

Who Was That?

Joash was one of the kings who ruled over the southern kingdom of Judah. The temple built by Solomon was getting old and needed to be repaired, so Joash did the work needed to make the temple beautiful again. Just as Joash honored God by repairing the temple, so can we honor God by what we do.

King Hezekiah and the People Worship God with Music

Bible-time people worshipped God in many different ways. Some worshipped God by gladly giving their offerings. Others worshipped God by reading and listening to his Word. (Everyone worshipped God by praying.)

People also worshipped God with music. David played a harp and sang to worship God. He also wrote the psalms, which are poems and songs to God. David wrote, "Sing to the Lord a new song," and "Make music to the Lord." King Hezekiah knew David had worshipped God with music, and Hezekiah wanted to do the same.

King Hezekiah ordered the priests and the musicians to come to the temple to worship God. The musicians came dressed in white and brought their instruments. Some played trumpets. Other musicians

brought cymbals, and some had harps to play. The musicians played their instruments while King Hezekiah and the people sang to worship God. They sang worship songs that King David had written. They sang, "Praise the Lord for he is good!" King Hezekiah and the people worshipped God with the sound and the words of their music.

To Remember

I will sing to the Lord. He has been so good to me.   Psalm 14:6

Ezra Rebuilds the Temple

The people who lived in Israel gathered together in Jerusalem to worship God. People came from their towns and villages all over the land. Some traveled a long distance to Jerusalem. They came because they loved God and wanted to worship him together.

The people told Ezra the priest to bring God's Word so he could read it to them. They wanted to listen to God's laws. The crowd that had gathered in Jerusalem was large. The people wanted to be sure they could hear Ezra read God's Word so they built a stage for Ezra to stand on.

When the stage was finished, the people gathered in front of it early in the morning. Ezra brought the scrolls of

To Remember
I will listen to what God the Lord will say.
Psalm 85:8

God's Word and stood on the stage. All the people could see him.

As Ezra unrolled the scroll, all the people stood up to show respect for God's Word.

When Ezra spoke, praising God for his words in the Scriptures, all the people agreed with Ezra and praised God for giving his Word.

Ezra read aloud from the scroll with God's Word from early in the morning until noon. All the people listened carefully while they stood all morning long.

Ezra and the people worshipped God by reading and listening to his Word.

Esther Takes a Stand

While the Israelites were held captive in Persia, a Jewish woman named Esther became queen.

Esther's cousin, Mordecai, refused to bow down to one of the king's men named Haman. Mordecai was a Jew and wouldn't dishonor God by bowing to any man. Haman became very angry and decided to pay back Mordecai.

That very day Haman sent orders to all parts of the empire to kill all the Jews.

When the Jews learned about Haman's plan, they began to cry. Mordecai, too, cried loudly outside the king's gate. Queen Esther sent a messenger to find out what was troubling Mordecai.

Mordecai told the messenger everything that had happened. He also gave the man a copy of Haman's orders to show Queen Esther. He told the messenger to urge her to go to the king and ask for mercy for her people.

Esther wanted to help, but there was one problem. If

she went to the king without having been invited, he could kill her!

After three days, Esther put on her royal robes and went to see the king. The king was happy to see her and held out his gold scepter to her. Esther invited the king and Haman to a banquet she was preparing.

At the dinner, the king asked Esther what she wanted.

Queen Esther answered, "If it pleases your majesty, please let me live. And please spare my people—this is what I want. My people and I have been sold to be killed."

The king was furious! "Who has dared

to do this?" he asked.

Esther pointed to Haman and said, "He's the one! He is the enemy of my people!"

Then Haman was terrified in front the king and queen. One of the king's servants said, "Haman was going to kill Mordecai—the man who helped you long ago—on a pole near his house."

The king said, "Put Haman to death!"

After Haman died, the king gave Mordecai a special place in the kingdom.

Then Queen Esther again went before the king. She asked him to let her people defend themselves, which the king granted. He issued a new law throughout all the land. Then the Jews defeated their enemies. They celebrated with a new holiday.

Esther was willing to say she was one of God's people even when it was dangerous to do so. She took a stand for God and saved her people.

To Remember
Save your people. Bless those who belong to you.   Psalm 29:9

Job Suffers

Job was the richest man in the land of Uz. He tried to live for God, and God blessed him.

Then one day everything was taken from him. His

children were killed in a great storm. He lost all his wealth. And to top it off, Job broke out with painful sores all over his body. But Job still held on to his faith. He wouldn't say anything bad about God.

Three of Job's friends came to comfort him. They thought Job had sinned. They were sure God was punishing him for that sin.

Job was honest about how he felt. He wondered why all this was happening to him. He wanted God to answer his complaints.

God talked to Job, reminding him that God was the one who had the power to create the world and the wisdom to know all things.

Job answered the Lord, "I'm not worthy. How can I reply to you? I'll stop talking."

Job saw a bigger picture of God. God went on to bless Job again. He gave him more children and twice as many riches as before.

To Remember

God, your saving acts reach to the skies. You have done great things. God, who is like you?
Psalm 71:19

Who Was That?

Job was a very rich man, but he loved God and tried to follow God's laws. Job taught his children to follow God too. But Job had some bad times. Sometimes bad things happen to us and we don't know why. When that happens to you, remember Job. He never understood why God let bad things happen. But he knew God was not confused, so Job kept his faith strong in the Lord. Remember, God always has a plan.

God Calls Isaiah

I saiah was a man who loved God.

One day God let Isaiah see him in a kind of dream. God was in a beautiful temple. He sat on a throne. His long robe filled the temple.

Angels were all around God. They were special angels called seraphs. They had six wings. Two were for flying, two covered their feet, and two covered their faces. They covered their faces and called out to each other, "Holy, holy, holy is the Lord who rules over all. The whole earth is full of his glory."

The temple shook and filled with smoke. Isaiah saw that God is holy. Isaiah felt awful about his sin. He cried, "I've sinned. I do wrong things and so does everyone else around me. Now I've seen you. I know you rule over everything." Isaiah knew how much God disliked sin.

One of the seraphs flew over to Isaiah. He held a hot coal from the altar with tongs. He touched Isaiah's mouth with the coal. The seraph told Isaiah God had forgiven his sin.

Then God said, "Who will tell others about me?"

Isaiah said, "Here I am. Send me!"

From that time on, Isaiah told God's message. He told people only God is holy and God hated the bad things they were doing. But he also told them how much God loved them and wanted them to love him too.

Some people listened to Isaiah, but most didn't. Those who did learned to love God more and more and to thank him for all the good things he had done.

To Remember

Holy, holy, holy is the Lord who rules over all.
The whole earth is full of his glory.
   Isaiah 6:3

God's Word Burns Up

God said to the prophet Jeremiah, "Write these words on a scroll: 'My people have not obeyed me. I will let their enemies destroy them if they do not choose to obey me.'"

Jeremiah told his helper, Baruch, to write God's words on a scroll.

Baruch wrote down the words and read the scroll to the people. Some of the people were afraid. They knew God's Word was true.

A man read God's words to the king. The king became angry and burned the scroll in a fire. He didn't want to believe God's Word was true.

God told Jeremiah to write the words again on a scroll. God said, "This country will not last. But my Word will last forever."

To Remember

Lord, your word lasts forever. It stands firm in the heavens.

Psalm 119:89

Daniel Eats Vegetables

A few years later, Nebuchadnezzar, the king of Babylon, captured Jerusalem and took many of the people to Babylon.

Nebuchadnezzar ordered his chief helper to pick some of the best young men to train for the king's service. He chose Daniel, Shadrach, Meshach, and Abednego.

The king wanted Daniel and the others to eat the best royal foods, but Daniel knew God would not be pleased by that. So he asked for only vegetables and water.

The servant didn't want to give Daniel and his friends just vegetables and water. He didn't think they would be healthy, and he was afraid the king would be angry and punish his servant for letting the men get sick.

So Daniel said, "Please test us for ten days. Give us nothing but vegetables and water. Then compare us with the young men who eat the king's food. See how we look. After that, do what you want to."

The king's servant agreed, and at the end of the ten days, Daniel, Shadrach, Meshach, and Abednego looked healthier than all the others, who had been stuffing themselves with the king's food!

Daniel and his friends honored God. And God honored them by giving them success in their work for the king.

To Remember

Eat and drink and do everything else for the glory of God.   1 Corinthians 10:31

Three Men Survive a Fiery Furnace

King Nebuchadnezzar built a huge, gold statue of himself. Then he called all the people together. His messenger said, "Whenever you hear the music, you must bow down and worship this statue. If you don't, you will be thrown into a blazing hot furnace."

So the people bowed when they heard the music. All the people except for Shadrach, Meshach, and Abednego.

The king was pretty upset when he heard about the men who wouldn't bow down! He

called for Shadrach, Meshach, and Abednego and said to them, "Is it true that you won't bow down to my statue? I'll give you another chance. But if you don't bow down, you will be thrown into the blazing hot furnace. Then no one will be able to save you."

The men said, "We will not bow down, O king. If you

put us into the blazing furnace, our God can save us. But even if he doesn't, we will not bow down to your statue."

Now the king was furious! He called for soldiers to throw the three into the furnace immediately!

The king sent his men to the furnace door. They threw the three men in.

Suddenly the king jumped up, amazed! He said to his helpers, "Didn't we throw three men in? Look! I see four!"

King Nebuchadnezzar called to the men, "You men who serve God Most High, come out!"

So Shadrach, Meshach, and Abednego walked right out. The fire hadn't hurt them, their clothes weren't black, and the men didn't even smell like smoke!

The king said, "Praise the one, true God! He has rescued his men!"

Then he made a new law: "No one can say anything bad about the God of the three brave men."

To Remember

Trust in the Lord and do good.   Psalm 37:3

A Hand Writes On a Wall

The new king of Babylon, King Belshazzar, had a huge dinner for all the important people in his kingdom.

As they drank from cups that belonged to God, they praised false gods made of gold, silver, wood, and stone.

Suddenly, fingers of a hand appeared and wrote a mysterious message on the wall.

The king called in his wise men to tell him what the words said, but the men didn't know. Then he sent for Daniel.

Daniel reminded the king of his father, Nebuchadnezzar. Nebuchadnezzar was very proud and didn't give God credit for helping him. One day, though, God took away his greatness. Nebuchadnezzar became like a wild animal until he admitted that God rules over everyone.

Daniel went on. "You know all of this, Belshazzar, but you are still proud. You praised your gods, but you didn't honor the one, true God. So he sent the hand that wrote on the wall."

Daniel told the king that the words said God was going to give Belshazzar's kingdom to another king.

Later that very night Belshazzar was killed, and Babylon was overthrown by some enemies. Belshazzar had not honored God, and he paid a huge price for it.

To Remember

Everyone on earth bows down to you [God]. They sing praise to you. They sing praise to your name.   Psalm 66:4

Daniel Lives with Lions

Just like the two kings before him, Darius, the new king in Babylon, respected Daniel and made him a top ruler in the land. This made some of the other rulers jealous. They didn't want Daniel to be so great.

They looked for ways to bring charges against Daniel, but Daniel always did things right.

Finally they realized they were going to have to be sneaky if they were going to catch Daniel doing something wrong. They knew he prayed to God three times each day, so they went to the king with an idea.

"King Darius, we have an idea," said one crafty man. "Make it a law that no one prays to anyone but you for thirty days. If they disobey this law, throw them into the lions' den."

The king didn't know Daniel prayed to God each day, and he liked the idea of people worshipping him, so he signed the law.

Daniel heard what the king had done, but he was faithful to God. So he did just as he had always done. He went to his upstairs room, opened his window toward

Jerusalem, got down on his knees, and gave thanks to God.

Some of the other rulers spied on Daniel and then ran to tell the king. "Daniel is not obeying your law," they said. "He still prays to his God three times a day."

The king was so upset by this news! He didn't want anything bad to happen to Daniel, so all day long he did everything he could to save him.

The mean, sneaky rulers reminded the king, "Remember, O king, no one—not even you—can change a law you make."

King Darius knew they were right, and he gave the order. Daniel was thrown into the lions' den.

The king said to Daniel, "You always serve your God

faithfully. So may he save you!"

A stone was placed over the opening of the den, and the king sealed it with his royal ring. Daniel was all alone in the dark with the lions.

King Darius went back to his palace, but he was so worried about Daniel that he couldn't eat or sleep.

As soon as it was light the next morning, the king rushed to the lions' den. "Daniel! Did your God save you?"

"My king, God sent his angel to shut the lions' mouths! They didn't hurt me at all!"

The king was so happy! He ordered his men to pull Daniel out of the den and to throw the sneaky rulers in!

Then the king wrote a new law. He ordered every person in his kingdom to respect and honor Daniel's God, the true God.

To Remember

Lord, teach me to follow your orders. Then I will obey them to the very end.   Psalm 119:33

Prayer Point

How would you feel if you were in danger as Daniel was? Remember, God created the lions and was in control of what they could do. When God saved Daniel he brought more praise to himself, and more people came to worship him! Thank you, God, for Daniel's example of faithfulness. Help me to be as brave as Daniel.

Love God First

During the same time Jonah was a prophet (we'll learn about him in the next story), the people of Israel felt pretty secure against their enemies. Times were good. But they had neglected God's law. They were doing all kinds of evil things. They forced poor people to pay for fair treatment when they went to court. They also hurt those who did right. They sold innocent people into slavery. And they worshipped idols.

So God sent a shepherd to be a prophet and preach against the evil in Israel. This prophet was named Amos, and he lived in a town called Tekoa.

God told Amos to boldly preach God's message to Israel: Turn from your evil ways or face God's punishment!

Being a prophet was not an easy job, but Amos did what God had told him to do.

A priest named Amaziah heard what Amos was preaching. He became angry! He went to King Jeroboam and lied about Amos. He made it sound like Amos was

trying to overthrow the king.

Finally, the priest told Amos to get out of his town and go home to Tekoa. "Don't bother us with your prophecies," he said.

Amos told Amaziah, "I'm not a trained prophet. I'm a shepherd. God called me away from my sheep and my fig trees to preach his message to you and the people of Israel.

"And now, because you wouldn't listen to God's message, bad things will happen to you, Amaziah."

Amos went on warning the people of Israel to turn back to God. Amos's message to the Israelites was clear: Hate evil, love good.

Amos warned that God's people would be scattered around the world. But God also promised Amos that a better day was coming. God would bring his people back to him and restore Israel to its former beauty and happiness.

TO Remember

Look to the Lord and live.   Amos 5:1

Jonah Swims with a Fish

onah heard God say, "Go to the city of Nineveh. Tell the people to love and obey me."

Jonah didn't want to go to Nineveh. He really didn't like the people there because they were enemies of the people in Israel. So Jonah chose to disobey God. He got on a boat going the opposite way! He thought he was pretty tricky, taking a boat going away from Nineveh. But God wasn't tricked. God knew what Jonah was doing.

Jonah went below deck to take a nap. God caused a big storm on the sea. The wind blew. Big waves crashed into the boat. The sailors were afraid the big waves and wind would make the boat fall apart.

The captain of the boat woke up Jonah. The captain said, "How can you sleep? Get up and pray that we won't die in this storm!"

The captain and the sailors thought Jonah might be part of the reason for the terrible storm. They asked Jonah who he was and why they were caught in the storm. When the sailors learned that he was trying to run

away from God, they said, "How could you do a thing
like that?"

Jonah said, "I know this storm is my fault. Pick me up
and throw me into the sea. Then the storm will stop." The
men didn't want to throw Jonah overboard. They were
sure he would drown. But they had no choice. And as
soon as Jonah was thrown overboard, the storm stopped!
And the sailors worshipped God.

Jonah didn't die in the sea. God sent a big fish to save him. The fish opened his mouth and swallowed Jonah whole!

From safe inside the big fish Jonah prayed to God. He thanked God for saving him. Jonah promised God he would obey.

After three days and nights, God made the fish cough up Jonah onto the beach.

Again God said, "Go to Nineveh and tell the people to love and obey me."

This time Jonah obeyed. He went straight to Nineveh. Jonah told the people everything God wanted them to hear. The people listened to Jonah and were sorry for not obeying God. They asked God to forgive them.

But Jonah wasn't happy. He didn't want God to show kindness to the people. So he walked up a hill outside the city, sat down, and pouted.

God wanted to help Jonah, so he made a large vine grow to give Jonah shade. Jonah was happy about the vine, but the next day, God sent a worm to chew up the vine. Jonah was angry that he didn't have shade anymore.

God said, "Jonah, you've been more worried about that vine than about all those people in Ninevah! I love those people and want them to know me."

God saved Jonah because God loved him even when he disobeyed. Jonah learned to obey God, and God was glad.

New TESTAMENT

An Angel Visits Mary

Mary was very excited because soon she would be getting married! The wedding was planned, and she looked forward to living with her new husband, Joseph.

One day God sent an angel to visit Mary. The angel said, "God has something special planned for you."

The angel's news upset Mary. She wondered what God's special plan was.

Then the angel said, "Do not be afraid, Mary. God is very happy with you. By God's power you will give birth to a son. You must name him Jesus. He will be God's Son. He will grow up to be great."

Mary asked how all of this could happen. The angel explained how God would work a miracle through her. The angel reminded Mary that nothing is impossible with God.

To Remember

Nothing is impossible with God.   Luke 1:37

Mary accepted what the angel had said. She wasn't afraid anymore. She said, "I am the Lord's servant." She was ready to do whatever God wanted her to do.

Did You Know?

Because people often had to travel a long way to attend a wedding, the ceremony usually lasted for three to seven days. The whole family was involved in the festivites. It was very different from the way we celebrate weddings today.

An Angel Visits Joseph

J oseph was a good man who had promised to become Mary's husband. They weren't married yet, but Mary was already carrying baby Jesus, God's Son, inside her body. God was working out his plan just like the angel had told Mary.

Joseph knew Mary was going to have a baby. He wasn't sure he wanted to get married to a woman who was going to have a baby before they were married. He began thinking about what he should do.

Joseph wanted to do what was good and right, so after much thought, Joseph decided to stop the wedding.

One night while Joseph was sleeping, God sent an angel to him in a dream.

The angel said, "Joseph, do not be afraid to take Mary home as your wife, because the baby inside her body is God's Son. She will have a baby boy. You are to name him Jesus, because he will save his people from their sins."

Joseph listened to what the angel said in his dream. Joseph remembered the instructions from God. In the morning, Joseph woke up and obeyed God. Joseph went to Mary and brought her home to be his wife. Now they were married. Joseph would name the baby Jesus, just as God had said.

To Remember

I won't waste any time. I will be quick to obey your commands.   Psalm 119:60

Who Was That?

Joseph, the man who married Mary and raised Jesus, was a descendent of King David. Mary, Jesus' mother, was also a descendent of King David. They were both a part of the promise God had made to Abraham long ago, when he promised Abraham that the Savior of all the world would be born to one of Abraham's relatives.

Joseph and Mary Welcome Baby Jesus

Joseph and Mary were married and living in the town of Nazareth. The time for Jesus to be born was coming close. About the same time the ruler of the land announced that everyone must go to the city his or her family was from to be counted. The government leaders required everyone to be counted so they could know who the people were.

Joseph's and Mary's families both came from the town of Bethlehem. It was not an easy time for Mary to travel because Jesus was about to be born, but they had to get to Bethlehem.

Once they were in Bethlehem, they went to the inn to get a room. But so many people had already come to Bethlehem that there was no room for Mary and Joseph in the inn.

What could they do? Where would Mary and Joseph find a place to stay?

Finally Joseph and Mary found a place to stay in a place like a stable. A stable is a shelter where animals were kept. In the stable were cows and sheep and a box

with straw for the animals to eat. The box was called a manger.

On the night Joseph and Mary stayed in the stable, Jesus was born.

They wrapped him in soft cloths. They held baby Jesus and loved him. Mary laid him in the manger. Joseph and Mary welcomed baby Jesus into their family.

In Ancient Days

There was no such thing as a hospital when Jesus was born. Mary and Joseph had to bring with them all the things they would need to take care of Jesus when he was born. But God had prepared Mary and Joseph so they could take good care of him. God's plans are so important that he doesn't leave anything to chance. We can trust him today, just as Mary and Joseph did 2,000 years ago.

To Remember

Today in the town of David a Savior has been born to you. He is Christ the Lord.

Luke 2:11

Angels and Shepherds Tell Good News

Shepherds around Bethlehem stayed out in the open fields at night with their sheep. Sometimes shepherds would join together to stay awake at night keeping their sheep together and safe from wild animals and thieves. The shepherds would talk with each other as they watched the sheep. They kept each other company during the long nights, and it made their work easier because they shared the work. It was important for the shepherds to watch that sheep didn't wander off and that no other animals hurt the sheep.

Usually the nights were quiet for the shepherds. Sometimes they had to chase away a hungry wolf or other wild animals, but not too much happened most nights. One night, however, things were not so quiet.

While the shepherds were tending the sheep, suddenly an angel of the Lord appeared in the sky! The shepherds were terrified!

The angel said, "Do not be afraid. I bring you good

news of great joy that will be for all people." The angel
told the shepherds about Jesus. He said, "Today in
Bethlehem a Savior has been born to you; he is Christ

the Lord." This meant that Jesus would grow up to save us from our sins. The angel also told the shepherds where to find Jesus and how to recognize him by saying, "You will find the baby wrapped in cloths and lying in a manger."

Suddenly the sky filled with a whole group of angels. They praised God, saying, "Glory to God in the highest, and on earth peace to everyone."

The angels left and went back to heaven. The shepherds said to each other, "Let's go to Bethlehem and see this thing that has happened, which the Lord has told us about." The shepherds hurried off and found Mary, Joseph, and Jesus. The shepherds found the baby just like the angels said, lying in the manger. The shepherds told everyone they saw about Jesus. The shepherds were so glad they could tell others the good news about Jesus' birth.

To Remember

May glory be given to God in the highest heaven! And may peace be given to those he is pleased with on earth!   Luke 2:14

Simeon Blesses Jesus

When Jesus was almost six weeks old, Mary and Joseph walked from Bethlehem to the temple in Jerusalem to give an offering and to thank God for Jesus.

An older man named Simeon lived in Jerusalem. He knew from God's Word that God would someday send a Savior for his people. God had told Simeon he would not die before he saw this Savior.

On the same day Mary and Joseph took baby Jesus to the temple, God let Simeon know he should go to the temple too. When Mary and Joseph walked into the temple area with Jesus, Simeon was there. God helped

Simeon know that the baby in Mary's arms was the Savior, God's Son.

Simeon was so excited! He had waited most of his life for this day. He went up to Mary and took Jesus into his arms. Simeon held Jesus and looked at the baby. As Simeon held Jesus in his arms, he prayed out loud to God. Simeon said, "Dear God, you have kept your promise to let me see your Son before I die. Thank you for helping me to know Jesus, your Son, who is the Savior for all of your people."

Mary and Joseph were amazed at what Simeon said about the child. Then Simeon spoke to Mary: "This child will grow up to be very important because of who he is."

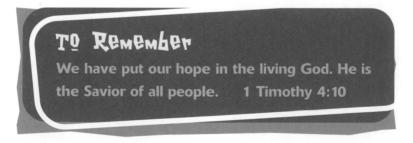

To Remember

We have put our hope in the living God. He is the Savior of all people.   1 Timothy 4:10

In Ancient Days

All Jewish babies were presented in the temple when they were forty days old. The priest recorded the baby's name and blessed the baby and the family. It was important for Jesus to fulfill all the laws of the Jewish people. So even when he was a baby, God made sure Mary and Joseph did everything that was required.

Wise Men Worship Jesus

When Jesus was born, God made a very bright star shine in the sky above Bethlehem. Wise men in a far eastern land watched the stars. When they saw the

bright star, these men knew it meant the King of the Jews was born. The men traveled to find the baby king and worship him.

The wise men stopped in Jerusalem to visit Herod, the king of the land. They thought he might help them find the baby king.

The wise men asked Herod, "Where is the one who has been born King of the Jews? We have come to worship him."

Herod didn't know about a King of the Jews who was born in his land.

He was angry! Herod wanted to be the only king in Israel.

Herod asked the temple leaders where the Christ was to be born. They told him Bethlehem. Now Herod knew where the wise men should search for Jesus.

Before Herod sent the wise men to Bethlehem, he said, "Go to Bethlehem and find this child," he said. "Then come tell me where he is so I can go worship too."

But Herod didn't really want to worship Jesus. Herod wanted to find out if this baby was really a king. He was afraid another king would try to take over his kingdom!

The wise men followed the star into the town of Bethlehem. Remember that Jesus was born in a stable because there was no room in the inn at Bethlehem. But Mary, Joseph, and Jesus didn't stay in the stable for long. They moved into a house in Bethlehem. When the wise men went into the house where the star stopped, they found Jesus. They opened their gifts of gold, incense, and myrrh and bowed down to worship him, Jesus the King.

To Remember

Lord, all of the nations you have made will come and worship you.   Psalm 86:9

God Takes Care of Jesus

After the wise men brought their gifts to Jesus, they were warned in a dream not to tell King Herod where Jesus was living. So they went home another way. But that didn't stop King Herod. He decided on a plan to kill all the baby boys that had been born around that time in Bethlehem.

One night God sent an angel to Joseph with a message: "Get up! It's not safe here. King Herod wants to kill Jesus. Go to Egypt until I tell you to come back."

Right then, Joseph got up. He woke Mary, and as quickly as they could, they got everything ready and took

Jesus away from Bethlehem.

The trip to Egypt was long and hard. The nights were cold, and the days were hot. But finally they arrived. Jesus was now safe, just as God said he would be!

Then, one night, a few years later, God's angel talked to Joseph again in a dream. The angel said, "Go back to your own land. King Herod is dead."

Again Joseph obeyed. As the family got closer to home, God warned Joseph that King Herod's son, the new king, was also mean. So Joseph, Mary, and Jesus went to Nazareth. Nazareth was a place where Jesus could grow up safe and happy. From Bethlehem to Egypt to Nazareth, God took care of Jesus.

To Remember

Save your people. Bless those who belong to you. Be their shepherd. Take care of them forever.   Psalm 29:9

Prayer Point

First, God told Joseph that Mary was going to have a baby boy, and Joseph listened. Then God told Joseph to take Mary and Jesus to Egypt so they would be safe. Thank you, God, that Joseph was such a good listener. He listened, and then he obeyed.

Jesus Gets "Lost"

Joseph, Mary, and Jesus lived in Nazareth. Jesus learned to work in Joseph's carpenter shop. Jesus would have started with small jobs. As he grew he would have learned to do more until he could make furniture

and other things from wood.

When Jesus was twelve, his family went on a trip from Nazareth to Jerusalem for the Passover celebration at the temple. Passover was the most important time of year for Jewish people.

Many families went to Jerusalem for Passover. They often traveled together in large groups because it was safer and more fun together.

After about four days of walking, Joseph, Mary, and Jesus, and all the other people from Nazareth came to the big wall around the city of Jerusalem. The city wall had a gate for people to go through the wall. Once inside, they could see the city and go to the temple.

During the next few days, the people sang, prayed, and listened to the older men teach about God.

When the days of worship and celebration ended, the people from Nazareth got together to start the four-day trip home. Joseph and Mary were part of this group. Jesus wasn't with Joseph and Mary, but they weren't worried. They knew he was probably with some of his friends somewhere in the large group of people going to Nazareth. But later in the day, Joseph and Mary couldn't find Jesus.

"Have you seen Jesus?" they asked. But no one had seen him.

Mary and Joseph hurried back to Jerusalem to look for Jesus.

They found him at the temple listening to the

teachers and asking them questions. The temple teachers were surprised at how much Jesus understood about God.

Mary said, "Oh, Jesus, we've been so worried about you."

Jesus said, "Didn't you know that I would want to be in my Father's house?" This was his way of saying he knew he was God's Son.

Mary and Joseph weren't sure what Jesus meant, but they didn't ask any more questions, and they didn't punish him.

Jesus went back to Nazareth with Mary and Joseph, and he obeyed them. Jesus grew wiser and stronger, and he pleased God as he continued to grow and learn.

To Remember

Listen to advice and accept what you are taught. In the end you will be wise.

Proverbs 19:20

John Baptizes Jesus

Jesus continued growing until he became a man. This was when Jesus began doing the work God had sent him to do. God sent Jesus to help people know about God and to be our Savior.

Jesus went to be baptized by a man named John. John was Jesus' cousin, and he spent his time traveling along the Jordan River, baptizing people and teaching them to follow God.

Everyone who came to John to be baptized had done bad things, except Jesus. Jesus had never done anything bad. He always pleased God.

John was baptizing other people when Jesus came to the Jordan River. Jesus went up to John and asked John to baptize him.

John recognized Jesus and knew he was God's Son. John said to Jesus, "I really should be baptized by you. Why are you coming to me?" John didn't think he was good enough to baptize Jesus.

But Jesus explained to John, "No, it is good and right for you to baptize me."

John accepted what Jesus said, and he baptized Jesus in the water of the Jordan River.

When Jesus came out of the river, an exciting thing happened. God sent his Spirit down on Jesus in the form of a dove. And the dove flew right to Jesus. Then God the Father spoke from heaven! God said, "This is my Son, and I love him. I am very pleased with him."

To Remember

John said, "Look! The Lamb of God! He takes away the sin of the world!"

John 1:29

Who Was That?

John was a cousin to Jesus. John's mother was named Elizabeth and his father was named Zechariah. Elizabeth and Zechariah were good friends to Mary and Joseph, and John was a good friend to Jesus. They were not only friends, they were family.

Matthew 4;
Mark 1; Luke 4

Jesus Chooses God's Way

Jesus wanted time to pray. So he went to the desert for forty days and forty nights.

The Devil wanted Jesus to do wrong. He said, "If you are God, turn this stone into bread."

Jesus was very hungry. He hadn't eaten in forty days! But he knew he needed to do what was right.

"That's not what God wants," Jesus said. "God's Word says we need more than bread to live. We need his Word."

The Devil took Jesus to a high place. He said, "Look at all the world. If you will worship me, I will give it all to you."

Jesus knew that wouldn't be right, either. It would be a sin to worship anyone but God.

"That's not what God wants," Jesus said. "God's Word says to worship only him."

So the Devil took Jesus to another high place. "If you are God's Son, jump off! God will save you, won't he?"

Jesus knew God loved him and would take care of him. But God wouldn't want him to do what the Devil asked.

"That's not what God wants," Jesus said. "God's Word says not to test God."

Then the Devil left Jesus alone, and the angels came to help Jesus.

Jesus had used God's Word to fight the Devil's temptations. He had not given in to them.

Prayer Point

The Devil tried the same lies with Jesus that he had used with Adam and Eve. He tried to confuse Jesus and make him say or do something that would be against God's will. But Jesus knew what God had written and what God wanted. Thank you, God, that your Word can protect us from the Devil's lies.

Jesus Teaches God's Word

When Jesus was about thirty years old, he left Nazareth to tell people throughout Israel about God, his heavenly Father.

But now Jesus had come back to Nazareth to visit and teach the people in Nazareth about God. The people were excited because Jesus was back in town.

It was a special day, the last day of the week, called the Sabbath. On the Sabbath people went to the synagogue to worship God. Jesus went too!

An important part of worship in a synagogue is someone reading aloud from God's Word. The person who read would always stand while reading God's Word.

This was a way to show respect for God's Word. After reading God's Word, the reader would sit down and explain what the words meant.

The day Jesus went to the synagogue in Nazareth, he was chosen to read a part of Scripture we have recorded in Isaiah 61. Jesus read God's Word to the people.

Isaiah 61 says God would send someone special to help all people know about God. This person would forgive people of their sins and heal them.

When Jesus finished reading God's Word, he said, "I am that special one God said he would send. God has sent me to help you know about him. I have come to forgive your sins and heal you."

The people didn't believe him! They were so angry they ran him out of town. They even tried to throw him off a cliff! But God protected Jesus, and Jesus walked right through the crowd and went on his way.

To Remember

He [God] has sent me [Jesus] to announce freedom for prisoners. He has sent me so that the blind will see again. He wants me to free those who are beaten down.   Luke 4:18-19

Luke 5;
Matthew 4

Jesus Says, "Follow Me"

Peter and Andrew had just been fishing, but they hadn't caught anything. They were on the shore cleaning and repairing their nets to be ready for the next

day of fishing. While they were working, Jesus was near-by teaching a crowd of people.

More and more people gathered around Jesus to hear him teach. Soon there were so many people that Jesus asked Peter to take him out a few feet from the shore in his boat so the people could hear him better.

When he finished teaching, Jesus told the crowd of people to go on their way. But Peter and Andrew stayed with Jesus.

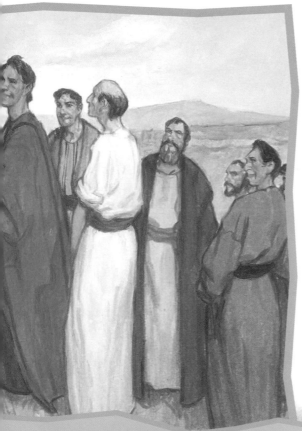

Jesus said, "Peter, row out to the deep water and throw out your net to catch some fish."

Peter said, "We put our net out all last night but didn't catch anything. We're tired! But I will put out the net because you say so."

Peter and Andrew threw out the net. When they

pulled it up, they were amazed to see so many fish in it!

The net was so full of fish that Peter and Andrew couldn't pull it into their boat. They had to call for help from their fishing friends, James and John.

Together the four fishermen pulled at the heavy net

until they dragged it up out of the water. There were so many fish that they filled both boats. The fishermen were surprised and delighted by how many fish they caught.

Jesus said, "Follow me and learn to fish for people." This was Jesus' way of saying he wanted the four men to become his disciples. Jesus wanted them to go wherever he went and learn from him. He wanted them to follow him so they would become more like him. Then they could help other people know about God.

The four fishermen rowed their boats to the shore and left the boats, nets, and fish to follow Jesus.

To Remember

"Come. Follow me," Jesus said. "I will make you fishers of people."
Matthew 4:19

Jesus Heals a Man With Leprosy

Leprosy is an awful skin disease. In Jesus' day, those with leprosy could not live with their families. They had to live in caves with other lepers. They could not go near other people. If anyone approached them, the lepers warned them by shouting, "Unclean! Unclean!" Most people who had leprosy were never cured. So they lived very lonely lives.

One day, a man with leprosy fell down on his face in front of Jesus.

He begged Jesus, "Lord, if you are willing, you can make me clean." Jesus knew the man was lonely and hurting. He reached out and touched the man, saying, "I'm willing. Be clean!"

That very minute, the man's leprosy was gone! His skin looked just like everybody else's!

The man was so happy, but Jesus warned him not to tell anyone. He said, "Go to the priest and do what God's

Word says. The priest and the people will see that you are clean."

But the men went out and told everybody he met what Jesus had done.

Soon, Jesus couldn't even go into a town without being surrounded by people. He stayed out in the lonely places, but people still came to hear him and to be healed by him.

Because people with leprosy were considered unclean, no one ever could touch them. But Jesus was willing to touch the man with leprosy, even when he could have healed him with just his word.

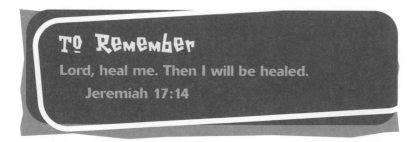

To Remember

Lord, heal me. Then I will be healed.
Jeremiah 17:14

Prayer Point

Leprosy was a terrible disease to have when Jesus walked the earth. It's just the same today, and there is still no cure. Thank you, God, that Jesus can heal our bodies as well as our souls.

Jesus Calls Matthew

Tax collector's right here! Everyone stop and pay your taxes before you go any farther!" Matthew shouted over the noise of people and animals passing by his tax collection booth.

People didn't want to pay Matthew, but they had to. It was the law. They paid even though they knew Matthew was getting rich by taking extra for himself. There was nothing they could do about it—except to not like Matthew. And that is what they did. They ignored him as much as they could, and when they spoke, they were never friendly.

Jesus was different. He cared about Matthew. Jesus went up to Matthew at his tax collection booth and said, "Follow me."

Without even thinking twice about it, Matthew left his job and went with Jesus.

People watched and thought, "What is Jesus doing?" They didn't like Matthew and thought Jesus shouldn't want to be around him. But Jesus did want to be with Matthew. Jesus cared for Matthew and everyone knew it.

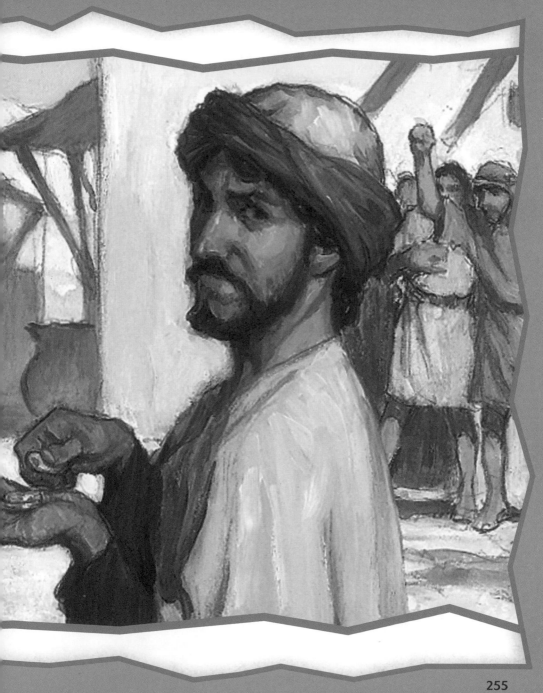

Jesus even went to Matthew's house for dinner. Most people would never eat with someone as bad as Matthew, but Jesus would.

Matthew invited more tax collectors and others who had done bad things. Matthew and his friends—men and

women most people didn't like—ate with Jesus.

The religious leaders were shocked when they found out Jesus was eating with Matthew and his friends. The leaders went to tell Jesus he shouldn't eat with a cheater like Matthew. They wanted to keep Jesus from liking Matthew. They were wrong. Jesus told them, "Healthy people don't need doctors. I didn't come to spend time with people who think they're right with God. I've come to get sinners to follow me."

To Remember

Jesus answered them, "Those who are healthy don't need a doctor. Sick people do. I have not come to get those who think they are right with God to follow me. I have come to get sinners to turn away fom their sins."
Luke 5:31-32

Jesus Heals on the Sabbath

It was the Sabbath day. God's commandment said the Sabbath should be a holy day to worship him. Jesus wanted to worship God at the synagogue.

The rulers of the synagogue did not like Jesus. "Let's see if Jesus breaks any of our rules for the Sabbath. Then we can get him in trouble," said one ruler to the others. Another ruler pointed to a poor man with a crippled hand.

"Maybe Jesus will heal that man's hand. That's against the rules. No work is allowed on the Sabbath."

The rulers went to Jesus and asked, "Is it right to heal someone on the Sabbath day? Isn't that work?"

Jesus answered, "If your sheep fell into a hole on the Sabbath, wouldn't you lift it out? A person is more important than a sheep. So it is right to do good on the Sabbath." Jesus said to the man with the crippled hand, "Put your hand out."

The man put his hand out. He could move his fingers and wave his hand. Jesus had healed him!

Jesus knew the right way to remember the Sabbath day. He worshipped God and helped other people.

To Remember

Remember to keep the Sabbath day holy.
Exodus 20:8

Prayer Point

The rulers of the synagogue thought it was more important to obey their rules than it was to obey God. But Jesus loved people so much that he wanted to help everyone that he could help. Thank you, God, that people are so important to you. Thank you for Jesus.

Four Friends Help

In the town of Capernaum lived a man who couldn't walk. He lay on his bed mat all the time.

Friends of the man heard Jesus had come to town. They were very excited. They knew Jesus could make their friend walk again!

The four friends were ready to help. The man's friends picked him up on his mat and carried him to the house where Jesus was teaching the people. But when they got there, they had a problem. There were so many people in the house listening to Jesus, the men couldn't even get through the doorway. There were even people standing outside looking through the windows.

"What shall we do?" they asked each other. "Jesus can heal our friend if we get him into the house."

Then one of them had an idea. They could carry their friend up the stairs on the outside of the house that led up to the flat roof.

Carefully the friends carried the man up to the roof and set him down. Then they dug through the thick hard clay of the roof to make an opening big enough for the man and his mat.

The four friends tied ropes to the corners of the mat.
Then they gently lowered their friend down through the
hole in the roof until he was right in front of Jesus.

Everyone was surprised to see a man coming down through a hole in the roof!

Jesus looked at the man. Then he looked up at the four friends who were looking down through the hole. Jesus knew these men believed he would make their friend well.

Jesus said to the man, "Stand up! Pick up your mat, and walk home."

Right then the man stood up. And he could walk! Everyone was very excited as they watched the man roll up his mat.

"Thank you, Jesus, for making me well," he said.

Then the man who was sick looked up at his four friends, smiled, and walked through the crowd to join his friends outside. The five men all walked home praising God for Jesus' power to heal.

To Remember

"I will give perfect peace to those who are far away and those who are near. And I will heal them," says the Lord.   Isaiah 57:18

Did You Know?

Sometimes we need help to do something hard, and sometimes we need friends to help keep our spirits up. Some people don't like to ask for help or to take help from someone. We think we have to do everything by ourselves. But God made us so that we are actually stronger and better when we have friends. God provides us with family members and friends who can help us. And we can help them, too!

Nicodemus Comes to Jesus

Nicodemus was a man who knew a lot about God and God's Word. But he wanted to know more. "I will go talk to Jesus," he said. "Jesus knows about God."

One night Nicodemus went to see Jesus. Nicodemus said to Jesus, "Teacher, you make sick people well. You make blind people see. I know you are from God."

Then Jesus said to Nicodemus, "If you want to be in God's family, you must become God's child."

"How can I become a child?" Nicodemus asked. "I am a grown-up man."

Jesus said to him, "You must become a new kind of person. It's like being a baby. Babies are new in a family. Now you must be a new part of God's family."

Jesus also said, "You can hear the wind, but you can't see the wind. That's what it is like when you come into God's family. You cannot see it happen, but God makes it happen.

"God sent his Son into the world as a person," said Jesus. "God's Son will die. He will die for all the bad things that people have done. But everyone who believes in God's Son will live forever in God's family."

Jesus wanted Nicodemus to be in God's family. Jesus wants everyone to be in God's family.

To Remember

God loved the world so much that he gave his one and only Son. Anyone who believes in him will not die but will have eternal life.

John 3:16

Jesus Meets a Woman at a Well

J esus and his disciples were traveling through the neighboring country of Samaria. They still had a long way to go, and it was a hot day for walking. About noon Jesus stopped to rest near a well. The disciples left Jesus alone at the well and went by themselves into a nearby town to buy some food.

While the disciples were gone, and Jesus was alone, a Samaritan woman came to get water from the well. She brought her jug to tie onto the rope and lower it down into the water. Then she would pull up the jug of water, untie it, and take the jug of water home.

Most people went to the well in the evening when the weather was cool. There they would get water and talk with each other about things that happened that day. But this woman went at noon so she wouldn't meet other people at the well. She was lonely and wanted to be left alone. She knew that most people didn't like her because of some things she did. Most people said mean things about her if they saw her, so she just avoided people when she could.

But Jesus cared for the lonely woman. He wouldn't say mean things about her. Jesus politely asked the Samaritan woman for a cup of water. But she just said, "I can tell you are a Jew and I'm a Samaritan. Our people don't get along, and yet you want me to give you a drink? Ha! How can you ask me for a drink?"

This was an angry and unexpected response to Jesus' request. But still, Jesus was kind.

While she was filling her water jug, Jesus asked, "Do you want me to give you living water?" This was Jesus' way of asking if she wanted to learn about forgiveness. Jesus wanted to forgive her sins.

"Sure! Let me have a drink of that water!" she replied. "Then I won't get thirsty and have to keep coming back to this well for more water. But how will you get some of that water out of this well? You don't have anything to put it in!" The woman didn't understand what Jesus was offering her.

Even when Jesus talked with the woman about things she did wrong, he didn't say anything mean to her like most people did when they saw her.

Finally the woman accepted Jesus' love and care for her. She knew that Jesus must be God's Son because he knew things about her no one else knew, and no one had ever cared for her the way Jesus did.

She ran back to town to tell others that she had met Jesus, the one who knows everything about us, forgives our sin, and cares for everyone.

To Remember

Lord, you have seen what is in my heart. You know all about me.   Psalm 139:1

Jesus Heals a Man Who Can't Walk

J esus came to a pool of water in Jerusalem called the Pool of Bethesda. It was one of many pools in the city where people would come to collect water to take home for drinking, cooking, and washing. Many people came to the pool every day.

Sometimes the water in the pool would bubble and make little waves in the water. People thought an angel from God made the water move. They believed the first person to get into the pool right after it moved would be healed of any illness or sickness he or she had. Every day people who had illnesses that couldn't be cured came to the pool. There were blind people, people who could hardly move, and some who couldn't walk.

These people spent their days at the pool of Bethesda. They would watch and listen for the water to move.

When Jesus came to the pool, he went up to a man who couldn't walk. The man was lying on a mat and had not walked for almost forty years. Jesus asked the man, "Do you want to get well?"

"Sir," the man replied, "I have no one to help me into the pool when an angel stirs up the water. I try to get in, but someone else always goes down ahead of me." He thought maybe he had found someone to help him get into the pool when the water moved. The man didn't know he was talking with Jesus.

Jesus said to him, "Get up! Pick up your mat and walk."

At once the man was healed. He picked up his mat and walked. Jesus moved away so quickly into the crowd of people at the pool, the man didn't even know the name of the one who healed him.

Some religious leaders from the temple saw the man walking with his mat. They wanted to know what had happened.

The man explained that a man at the pool had healed him and told him to pick up his mat and walk.

The leaders asked, "Who told you to do this?"

The man said, "I don't know his name."

Later Jesus found the man in the temple. Jesus talked with him. Then the man knew who healed him. The man told everyone that Jesus had healed him.

To Remember

Lord, I wait for you to help me. Lord my God, I know you will answer.

Psalm 38:15

Jesus Chooses His Disciples

God sent his Son Jesus to tell people about God. Jesus healed the sick, died on a cross, and came back to life, so people would know God is good and loves us. Many people learned about God because of what Jesus did and taught. One thing Jesus taught is that we can ask God for help. One way he taught us is by his own example.

Jesus wanted some special helpers to be his disciples. They would follow Jesus and learn from him.

The disciples would teach people about God after Jesus went back to heaven.

The night before Jesus picked his disciples he prayed to God in heaven. He wanted his Father's help in making such an important decision. He prayed all through the night.

In the morning, Jesus called twelve men to follow him and be his disciples. The disciples' names were Simon

Peter, Andrew, James, John, Philip, Bartholomew, Matthew, Thomas, James the son of Alphaeus, Simon the Zealot, Judas the son of James, and Judas Iscariot. One at a time Jesus picked each of these men. One by one they went and stood with Jesus. They became his twelve disciples.

Jesus asked God to help him pick his disciples. We can follow Jesus' example by asking God to help us.

Another time Jesus said, "Ask and it will be given to you." Jesus wants us to know that God is good and will give good things to people who ask.

To Remember

Ask, and it will be given to you. Search, and you will find. Knock, and the door will be opened to you.   Matthew 7:7

Who Was That?

The disciples Jesus called were very special. They kept on teaching about Jesus even though it was against the law. Those twelve men Jesus called when he first started preaching helped spread God's Word all over the earth. We can do the same thing today by talking about God's kingdom wherever we go.

God Cares for Us

J esus went out on a hill and found a place to sit in a field. The disciples and a large group of people sat on the ground where they could listen to Jesus teach.

Jesus said, "Do not worry. Don't worry about your life and what you will eat or drink. And don't worry about what you will wear. God knows what you need."

Jesus helped the people understand what he was teaching. He explained, "Look at the birds of the air. They don't plant seeds or gather crops and store food in barns. But God knows what they need and feeds them." Jesus went on to say that we are much more valuable to God than the birds. If God knows that the birds need food, then he surely knows that we need food.

Jesus and the people were sitting in a field of beautiful flowers. He said, "Look at the flowers in this field. They don't worry about what they will wear. They don't spend their days working so they can buy clothes. But the flowers look nicer than a rich king in very fine clothes. God in heaven dresses all the plants in the fields. You are much more important to God than flowers."

Jesus said, "Do not worry, saying, 'What will we eat?'

or 'What will we drink?' or 'What will we wear?' People who don't know me worry about these things. They become so busy with trying to get what they need that they don't have time for what is important to God. Don't worry like they do; God knows what you need."

To Remember

Your heart will be where your riches are.
Luke 12:34

Two Men Build Houses

esus wanted to show people how they could build strong, happy lives by listening to his words and obeying them. He also wanted the people to know what could happen if they ignored his words. So Jesus told a story about two men who built houses.

The first man, a wise man, found a big rock and built his house on it. When a storm came, it rained hard and the wind blew. The storm was frightening! The water rose higher and higher around the house. The walls shook. But the house stood strong; it didn't fall. The man's house was safe and secure.

The second man, a foolish man, also built a house. But this man built his house on the sand.

When a storm came, it rained hard and the wind blew. The water rose higher and higher around the house.

The walls cracked and broke! The man's house on the sand fell down with a loud crash.

Jesus said that the man who built his house on the rock was like the people who hear God's Word and do what God says. They will find strength during hard times. The man who built his house on sand was like the people who hear God's Word, but don't do what it says. Life will be much more difficult for them.

To Remember

Don't just listen to the word. You fool yourselves if you do that. You must do what it says.

James 1:22

Jesus Heals a Little Girl

Jairus worried about his daughter. She was very sick, and the doctors said she would die soon. There wasn't any time to waste. He had to do something fast.

Jairus had heard about Jesus and the miracles he had done. He knew Jesus was the only one who could help. So Jairus hurried away to see Jesus.

When he saw Jesus, he fell to his knees. "Please come," he begged. "My little girl is dying. Place your hands on her to heal her. Then she will live."

Jesus cared about Jairus and his daughter and was sad she was so sick. He decided to heal her.

It wasn't easy to leave. So many people wanted to see Jesus that they crowded around him. He couldn't leave very quickly.

And before Jesus could go, a woman who also was sick came up to him. She had been bleeding for twelve years. She had spent all her money trying to get better, but nothing had worked.

Like Jairus, she had heard Jesus could heal. She thought, "I just need to touch his clothes. Then I'll be healed." So she touched Jesus' clothes—and her bleeding stopped that very second!

Right then, Jesus knew God's power had gone through him. He asked, "Who touched me?"

Even though she thought Jesus might be mad, she told him everything.

Jesus wasn't upset. He said, "Dear woman, your faith has healed you. Go in peace."

Just then, some people came from Jairus's house. "Your daughter is dead," they said. "Don't bother the teacher anymore."

"Don't be afraid," Jesus told Jairus. "Just believe."

They went to Jairus's home and saw everyone crying.

Jesus asked, "Why all this sadness and crying? The child isn't dead. She's only sleeping."

Everyone laughed at Jesus because they knew the little girl was dead. But they didn't know the power of God.

Jesus made everyone leave the house except the girl's parents. He took her hand and said, "My child, get up!"

The litttle girl's spirit came right back to her. She stood up and walked around!

Jairus and his wife were so happy Jesus had healed their daughter! Many people didn't believe he could, but Jairus did.

TO Remember

The way to do what God requires must begin by having faith in him.

Romans 10:6

A Boy Shares His Lunch

I see Jesus! There he is!" a child called. Everywhere Jesus went, people came to hear him teach about God's love. They knew he was someone special and that he had important things to say about God.

One day more than five thousand people gathered to hear Jesus. All day the crowd listened.

Late in the afternoon Jesus knew the people were hungry. Jesus asked Philip, one of his disciples, "Philip, where shall we buy food for these people to eat?"

Philip said, "There are thousands of people here. We don't have enough money to buy them even a little food."

Another helper named Andrew said, "Here is a boy who wants to share his lunch, but it isn't enough to feed this crowd." The boy walked up to Jesus carrying his lunch basket.

What was in the boy's lunch basket? One, two small fish. One, two, three, four, five small loaves of bread. This was lunch for one child. Jesus needed food for more than five thousand people!

The boy didn't know how Jesus would feed all those people with his two fish and five loaves of bread, but Jesus did.

Jesus told his disciples, "Have all the people sit down."
The boy gave his lunch basket to Jesus. He stood close by

while Jesus prayed to thank God for the food.

Then Jesus began handing out fish and bread to the people. He gave food to one thousand people. There was still plenty of food. He handed bread and fish to two thousand people, and then three thousand people. There was still more food. There were more than five thousand people that day who ate as much as they wanted. The little boy watched as people ate the lunch Jesus helped him share.

Then Jesus said to his disciples, "Gather up all of the leftovers so nothing will be wasted." When the disciples finished collecting the leftovers, everyone was surprised that there were still twelve baskets of bread and fish.

The boy was glad Jesus helped him share his lunch.

To Remember

The godly are always giving and lending freely. Their children will be blessed.

Psalm 37:26

Peter Walks on Water

Jesus was teaching his disciples and a large crowd of people near the Sea of Galilee. Late in the afternoon, he told his disciples to get into a boat and go across the water to the other side.

As the sun went down, the disciples rowed across the Sea of Galilee, the people walked home, and Jesus went up on the side of a hill by himself to pray.

Jesus prayed all night. The disciples were in the boat all night too. They had come up against a storm. Even though they rowed very hard, the wind and the waves kept pushing against them. They were a long way from the land out on the water, but Jesus knew where his disciples were and the hard time they were having.

Very early in the morning before the sun came up Jesus went out to the disciples. Jesus didn't take a boat; he walked on top of the water! When the disciples looked up and saw Jesus walking on the water, they were terrified! They thought he was a ghost!

Jesus called out to them, "Don't be afraid. It's me."

Peter wanted to be sure so he said, "Lord, if it's really you, tell me to come to you on the water."

Jesus said, "Come, Peter." Jesus wanted Peter to trust him.

Peter climbed out of the boat, trusting Jesus to help him walk on the water. One step after another, Peter walked on the water by God's power.

Just before Peter got to Jesus, he looked at the storm clouds. He listened to the wind whipping the sails, and he felt the cold spray of the waves. Peter became afraid and stopped trusting Jesus to help him walk on the water. He began to sink.

Peter cried out, "Lord, save me!"

Right away Jesus reached out his hand and caught

Peter. Jesus said, "You trusted me for a while. Why did you stop?"

Jesus helped Peter back into the boat. The wind and waves stopped. Peter and the other disciples in the boat worshipped Jesus because they understood more about his love and greatness. They were learning that they could trust Jesus and that he wanted them to trust him.

To Remember

Lord, those who know you will trust in you. You have never deserted those who look to you.
Psalm 9:10

Matthew 15;
Mark 7

Jesus Heals a Woman's Daughter

One day a woman came to see Jesus. She cried to him, "Lord! Have mercy on me. An evil spirit controls my daughter."

Jesus didn't answer her. His disciples wanted to send her away. They thought she was bothering Jesus.

The woman kept crying out to Jesus.

Jesus said, "I was sent only to the people of Israel."

But the woman kept asking for help. She knew Jesus could heal her daughter!

Then Jesus said, "You have great faith! You will be given what you are asking for." And Jesus healed her daughter at that moment.

To Remember
Everything is possible for the one who believes.
Mark 9:23

297

Jesus Teaches How to Forgive

Peter came to Jesus with a question. He wanted to know what to do when someone did something wrong to him. "Jesus, how many times should I forgive someone who is mean to me? Is seven times enough?" he asked.

Jesus said, "Not seven times, but seventy-seven times." That was Jesus' way of saying, "Just keep on forgiv-

ing. Don't even count how many times you forgive others." Then Jesus told this story to help Peter learn that to love means to keep on forgiving.

Once there was a king. The king had a servant who owed him millions of dollars. The king told his servant, "I want my money back. Pay me now."

The servant couldn't repay the king because he didn't have enough money.

The king said, "You and your wife and your children and everything you own must be sold to repay me!"

The servant got on his knees and begged, "Please, please give me more time to pay you back. I will work hard and repay everything you loaned to me!"

The king felt sorry for his servant and changed his mind. He told the servant to stand up. The king said, "I forgive you. You won't ever have to pay me back." The servant no longer owed any money! He went away happy that he was forgiven.

Soon after this, the servant who was forgiven saw one of his friends who owed him only a few dollars. The servant grabbed his friend and shouted, "Pay back all the money you owe me right now!"

The friend begged, "Please, please give me more time to pay you back. I will work hard and pay back everything I owe you!"

But the servant didn't feel sorry for his friend and wouldn't forgive him. The servant had his friend thrown into jail until he could repay the money. The servant wouldn't forgive like the king did.

The king heard what happened. He immediately asked to see the servant. He said, "When you owed me millions of dollars, I forgave you. But when someone owed you just a few dollars, you wouldn't forgive him. Now you will go to jail because you didn't forgive someone like I forgave you."

Then Jesus said, "This is how God feels about forgiving others."

Did You Know?

 Jesus liked to tell stories that would help people understand about God. Today we call those stories parables. Jesus knew how hard it was to forgive someone who is mean to you. He told this story so we would learn to be like him and keep on forgiving.

To Remember

Put up with each other. Forgive the things you are holding against one another. Forgive, just as the Lord forgave you.

Colossians 3:13

Jesus Spots a Trap

All Jewish people were forced to give taxes to the Roman government. There were taxes on crops, taxes on houses and lands, and taxes on the money people earned. These taxes always reminded the Jewish people that they belonged to Rome, and Caesar was their king. The Jewish people, however, would never agree that they belonged to anyone but God.

One day, the religious leaders tried to trap Jesus. They knew he would have to say something bad about Rome or about God. Either way, he'd be in big trouble!

The men asked him a question: "Teacher, is it right to pay taxes to Caesar?"

Jesus knew exactly what they were trying to do. They weren't fooling him one bit! He said, "You pretenders! Bring me the coin used to pay the tax."

They brought him a coin.

Jesus held it up and asked, "Whose picture is on this coin? Whose words are on this coin?"

"Caesar's," they replied.

Then he said to them, "Give to Caesar what belongs to Caesar. And give to God what belongs to God."

Jesus' answer totally amazed the people who tried to trick him. Instead of arguing against taxes, Jesus showed that people need to obey those in charge. Jesus expects his followers to give him their highest loyalty and worship, but he also wants us to respect those who are placed in charge of us.

To Remember

Remind God's people to obey rulers and authorities. Remind them to be ready to do what is good. Titus 3:1

Three Men Handle Money

Jesus told a story about three servants. The master gave each servant the amount of money he knew the servant could take care of. He gave one $10,000. He gave another $4,000. And he gave the third $2,000. Then he left on a trip.

After a long time the master returned. He called his servants together to see what they had done with his money.

The man who had received the most money spoke first. "Master," he said, "look! Your money has earned ten times more!"

His master replied, "Well done! Now I know I can trust you with even more!"

The man with the $4,000 also came. "Master," he said, "look! Your money has earned five times more!"

His master replied, "Well done! Now I know I can trust you with even more!"

Then the third servant came forward. "Master," he said, "I was afraid I might lose your money, so I buried it."

The master replied, "That was a terrible idea!" Then he said to another servant, "Take his money away from

him and give it to the servant with the most money. I can't trust this man with even a little!"

Jesus wanted his listeners to use whatever God had given them for him.

To Remember

God made us. He created us to belong to Christ Jesus. Now we can do good things.

Ephesians 2:10

God Remembers How We Treat Others

Jesus was outside on a hillside teaching his disciples. He talked about some things that will happen in the future. Jesus said that someday he will sit on a heavenly throne as the King of heaven and earth. He will bring all the people of the world to him. From his throne Jesus will separate all of the people into two groups, one on each side.

Jesus said he will talk to one group first. He will say, "When I was hungry and thirsty you gave me food and water. When I was alone and didn't have a friend, you became my friend and invited me to your house. I needed clothes and you gave me new clothes. When I was sick

you took care of me. When I was in jail, you came and visited me."

Then the people in the first group will say, "Lord, we don't remember feeding you when you were hungry. When did we see you thirsty and give you something to drink? We also don't remember inviting you to our houses or giving you clothes. When did we see you sick or in prison and go to visit you?"

Then Jesus will explain that he kept track of how they treated others. Jesus will say, "Everything you did to others, you did to me." This means that when they gave food or something to drink to a person, it was like they gave food or a drink to Jesus.

God keeps track of how we treat others because everyone is important to him. He keeps track of the kind

things we do and also the mean things that hurt people. Jesus cares so deeply about every person that he feels what people feel. It is as if everything we ever do to others, whether it is kind or mean, we also do the same to Jesus.

Jesus wants us to know that God expects us to show that we love others. When we treat others well, we show them what God's love is like. God keeps track of how we treat others because what we do to others matters to him.

The other group will be those who didn't treat others well or didn't ask Jesus to forgive them for mistreating others.

We all do some things wrong. Sometimes we don't treat people like we should. When we ask Jesus to forgive us for the wrong things we do, he will forgive us. When Jesus forgives us, he chooses to not remember what we did wrong. He doesn't keep track of it anymore. He forgives us because he loves us.

To Remember

[Jesus said,] "Anything you did for one of the least important of these brothers of mine, you did for me."   Matthew 25:40

Did You Know?

It is very important to God how we treat other people. God loves all of us so much. It hurts him when we are mean to each other. We can choose to be like Jesus and be kind to people and help them. That makes him very happy.

Jesus Teaches Prayer

Jesus often talked with God his Father. When Jesus prayed, he gave all his attention to God and showed respect for him. Jesus knew God loved him and always listened to his prayers. He knew God would answer his prayers.

One day after Jesus finished praying, one of his disciples said to him, "Lord, teach us to pray."

Jesus taught his disciples (and us) to call God "Father" because God is like a father to all who love him.

Jesus taught that when we pray, we first should praise God. We praise God in a prayer by telling him how great he is. The first part of the prayer Jesus prayed is, "Father, may your name be honored."

Jesus also taught us to remember that our food comes from God. He said, "Give us each day our daily bread."

Jesus knew we would do some things wrong, so he prayed, "Forgive us our sins."

Jesus taught us to ask God to help us say no to bad things, so he prayed, "Keep us from falling into sin when we are tempted."

Jesus also taught his disciples that God loves us and wants to answer our prayers. He said, "If your son asked you for a fish to eat, would you give him a snake? If he asked for an egg, would you give him a stinging scorpion?" Jesus knew no loving father would give his child anything that

might cause harm. He wanted his disciples to know that our heavenly Father wants to give us good things.

God loves us and always listens to our prayers. He will answer our prayers. Jesus taught us this prayer so we would know how to pray to our loving God.

TO Remember

Jesus said to them, "When you pray, this is what you should say, 'Father, may your name be honored. May your kingdom come. Give us each day our daily bread. Forgive us our sins, as we also forgive everyone who sins against us. Keep us from falling into sin when we are tempted.'"

Luke 11:2-5

Jesus Helps a Man Believe

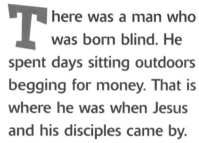

There was a man who was born blind. He spent days sitting outdoors begging for money. That is where he was when Jesus and his disciples came by.

Jesus spit on the dirt and made some mud. He put the mud on the man's eyes. Jesus told him, "Go wash in the Pool of Siloam."

The blind man obeyed Jesus. Then he could see for the first time in his whole life. He jumped for joy and shouted, "I can see! I can see!" Then he ran to see his family for the very first time.

The neighbors asked,

"Isn't this the same man who used to sit and beg?"

Other people said, "No. He only looks like him."

But the man who had been blind said, "I am the man who used to sit and beg." He explained, "The man they call Jesus really did make me see."

The religious leaders wanted to know how the man who was born blind could see. They didn't believe Jesus had made him see. But the man knew that Jesus had healed him.

Later that day, Jesus found the man he had healed. Jesus asked, "Do you believe in God's Son?" The man said, "Who is he? Tell me so I may believe in him." Jesus said, "I'm Jesus, God's Son."

That was all that Jesus needed to say. The man said, "Lord, I believe." He knelt down and worshipped him because he believed in Jesus.

TO REMEMBER

Jesus [said,] "I am the light of the world. Those who follow me will never walk in darkness."
John 8:12

Jesus Is the Good Shepherd

In Bible times there were many men whose job it was to take care of sheep. These men were called shepherds. To help people learn about how much he loves them, Jesus talked about the work that a good shepherd does for his sheep.

A shepherd has a sheep pen where he keeps his sheep safe at night. The only way the sheep can get into the sheep pen is by going through the one opening. During the night the shepherd stays at the door of the sheep pen so none of the sheep can wander out. The shepherd won't let any strangers come through the door or climb over the wall to steal a sheep.

In the morning, the shepherd calls his sheep to come follow him. They come because they know their shepherd's voice and they listen to him. The shepherd leads the sheep and the sheep follow him. The sheep know him and they know that he will take care of them.

The shepherd stays with his sheep all day long. He takes them to water and green grass. He might carry the young ones when they are tired. If a wolf comes to

attack the sheep, the shepherd will stay with his sheep to protect them. He will do everything necessary to keep the wolf from hurting his sheep.

Everything the shepherd does is for his sheep. He gives up his life every day to care for his sheep because they belong to him.

The people already knew everything Jesus told them about the work a shepherd does for his sheep. But Jesus wanted them to understand how much he loved them. So he explained, "Just like there is only one door into a sheep pen, there is only one way into heaven. I am the only way into heaven. You must believe in me to get into heaven."

Jesus also said, "I am the Good Shepherd. The people who follow me are like my sheep. I lay down my life for my sheep. They are important to me because they belong to me."

Just as the shepherd loves and cares for his sheep, Jesus loves and cares for each of us.

To Remember

"I am the good shepherd. I know my sheep, and my sheep know me."   John 10:14

In Ancient Days

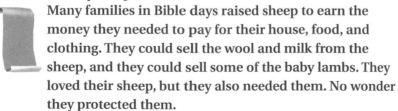

Many families in Bible days raised sheep to earn the money they needed to pay for their house, food, and clothing. They could sell the wool and milk from the sheep, and they could sell some of the baby lambs. They loved their sheep, but they also needed them. No wonder they protected them.

Parable of the Rich Man

I n the Ten Commandments God tells us not to steal and not to covet—to wish for or be jealous of the good things that others have.

When Jesus taught the people, he warned them not to be greedy, because there's more to life than having lots of money and things. To help the people understand what he meant, Jesus told a story about a rich man.

The land of a certain rich man produced a big crop. His barns were overflowing! So he said to himself, "I don't have enough space to store all this grain. I'll tear down my barns and build bigger ones. I can put my crops and all my other things inside. Then I don't have to work anymore! I can just relax and take life easy!"

The rich man didn't think about people who had nothing to eat. He didn't think about God, who had given him all his riches. He only thought of himself and enjoying life.

That very night the man died, and all his crops and money went to waste. He would never enjoy all the things he had stored in his big barns. Even worse, he hadn't shared, and he hadn't thanked God for any of it.

Jesus told the people that money and possessions don't make people happy.

Only God can give true riches—blessings that can never be stolen or lost.

T͚ Reme7mber

Put God's kingdom first. Do what he wants you to do. Then all of those things will also be given to you.   Matthew 6:33

Jesus Tells About Shepherds

One day Jesus told a story about a sheep and a shepherd to teach us about his love. Here is how the story went.

Once there was a shepherd. This shepherd had one hundred sheep to take care of!

The shepherd loved each of his sheep. Every morning he led the sheep to fields where they could eat fresh green grass. Near the end of each day, the shepherd brought the sheep home to be safe.

Every night the shepherd counted the sheep to be sure he hadn't lost any. He counted, "One, two, three, four..." He kept counting until at last he was near the end. "Ninety-six, ninety-seven, ninety-eight, ninety-nine—I should have one hundred sheep. Oh no, one of my sheep is lost!"

After he made sure the ninety-nine sheep were safe, the shepherd went to look for the one lost sheep. He loved all of his sheep, including the lost one.

The sun went down and it got dark and cold, but still the shepherd looked. He looked everywhere. He just couldn't go to sleep until he found his lost sheep. He went back to the field of green grass where the sheep had spent the day. The lost sheep wasn't there. He looked behind rocks, but he didn't find the lost sheep there, either.

Then at last the shepherd heard a familiar sound. He followed it across the field, until finally he came to a hole. There was the lost sheep!

The shepherd reached down, gently picked up the sheep, and carried it back home. He put the sheep that was lost with the other ninety-nine in the sheep pen. Now all his sheep were together where he could protect them. The shepherd was so happy that he called his friends and neighbors and said, "Come to a party. Celebrate with me because I found my lost sheep!"

God loves us so much he will search for us, just like the good shepherd loved and searched for his sheep.

To Remember

The Son of Man [Jesus] came to look for the lost and save them.   Luke 19:10

A Selfish Son Comes Home

J esus told this story to teach people about God's forgiveness.

There was a man who had two sons. One day, the younger son came to his father and said, "I don't want to wait any longer. I want my share of the family money now."

The father was sad, but he didn't argue. Instead, he took the family money and divided it between his two sons.

The young man took all his money and went far from home. Instead of using his money wisely, he spent it on wrong things for himself and his friends.

Before long, the young man had spent all his money. "Oh no," he cried, "I have no more money! I have nothing to eat! What am I going to do?"

Finally, the young man found a job. Someone hired him to go out in the fields and feed the pigs. He was so hungry that he would have gladly eaten the pigs' food. But no one gave him anything.

Then he came to his senses and began to think

smarter. He said to himself, "The people who work for my father have more than enough food! But here I am dying from hunger! I'll go back to my father. I'll say to him, 'Father, I've done wrong things. You and God didn't want me to do them. I don't deserve to be called your son. Make me like one of your workers.'"

So the young man quit his job feeding pigs and walked back to his father's home.

While the son was still a long way off, his father looked up and saw him coming. The father was full of love for his son. He didn't even wait for his son to come to him. Instead, the father ran out to meet his son.

He threw his arms around him and hugged and
kissed him.

The son said, "Father, I have done wrong. I don't
deserve to be called your son."

But the father didn't think about all his son had done
wrong. He forgave his son and was glad that he had
come home.

"Quick!" the father told his servants. "Bring the best clothes in the house and put them on my son. Put a ring on his finger and sandals on his feet. Let's have a big dinner to celebrate. This son of mine was lost, but now he has come home."

The family servants did everything the father had said. They helped his son get cleaned up and got him some new clothes. And together they had a big "Welcome Home" party to celebrate that his son was home and back with the family.

To Remember

It is the same in heaven. There is joy in heaven over one sinner who turns away from sin.
Luke 15:10

Jesus Raises Lazarus from the Dead

A messenger told Jesus some sad news. He said, "Lord, your good friend Lazarus is sick."

Jesus loved Lazarus and his sisters, Mary and Martha. But Jesus didn't go to Lazarus right away. He waited two days.

Then Jesus said to his disciples, "Let's go to Bethany where Lazarus is." Jesus told them he knew Lazarus had died from the sickness, but he would use the situation to help people believe in his love and greatness.

Jesus and the disciples walked to Bethany. When they were just outside town, Martha ran to meet Jesus. She said, "Lord, I wish you would have come sooner. Then Lazarus wouldn't have died!"

Mary also came to see Jesus. She said, "Lord, I wish you had been here. Then my brother would not have died." Mary and Martha were crying because Lazarus was dead. They didn't think Jesus could help now.

Jesus cried too, because he loved Lazarus. He asked,

"Where have you put your brother's body?"

Mary and Martha took Jesus to the tomb where Lazarus was buried. It was in a cave with a large stone over the opening.

Jesus said, "Take the stone away from the cave."

"But, Lord," Martha said, "By now there is a bad smell. Lazarus has been dead four days!"

Jesus said to Martha, "If you believe, you will see the power of God."

Jesus' disciples and some other people pushed the stone away from the cave. Then Jesus prayed out loud to his Father in heaven. Jesus thanked God for always hearing him. Then Jesus said in a loud voice, "Lazarus, come out!"

Lazarus walked out of the cave! His hands and feet were wrapped with strips of cloth. Jesus said, "Take off the grave clothes and let him go."

Mary and Martha were so happy that Jesus made Lazarus alive again!

Many others who knew Lazarus, Mary, and Martha saw Jesus bring Lazarus back to life. Some people heard others tell them how Jesus raised Lazarus from the dead. Many of the people who saw Jesus and heard about Lazarus put their faith in Jesus.

To Remember

Jesus said..., "I am the resurrection and the life. Anyone who believes in me will live, even if he dies." John 11:25

Did You Know?

Because the land where Jesus lived was very rocky, people who died were often buried in caves or tombs cut into the rock. Sometimes a family would have many caves that they used, and those caves would be used for many generations. Several years after someone had died and been buried, they would collect the bones of that person and put them in a very special jar. Then after a while, another person could be placed in the same tomb. The Jewish people are still very respectful of how they treat their family members when they die.

Jesus Loves the Children

It was a beautiful, sunny day. Many people from all around had come to see Jesus. They came to hear about God's love. Everyone sat on the grass and listened to Jesus. There were many children in the group. They sat quietly with their parents and listened to Jesus too.

After a while there was time for the children to run and play. Then some of the moms and dads had an idea. They wanted to bring their children to Jesus so he could talk with them, hold them, and bless them. So some of the parents walked toward Jesus, carrying their babies. Others led their children by the hand to meet Jesus.

When the parents and children came closer to Jesus, the disciples saw them starting to crowd around Jesus. The disciples didn't want them to bother Jesus, so they told the parents to go away.

The disciples thought they were doing a good thing, but they weren't. Jesus saw what his disciples were doing. He wanted to see the children. Jesus said, "Let the little children come to me."

The disciples stepped out of the way. The children ran to Jesus. No one stopped Jesus from being a good friend.

While Jesus held the children, he said to all the people, "Everyone must trust in me in the way these children do. Learn from them how to love me."

Jesus hugged the children, put them on his lap, and held them in his arms. Jesus prayed for them and spent time with them. They all knew Jesus was their friend.

To Remember

Jesus said, "Let the little children come to me. Don't keep them away. The kingdom of heaven belongs to people like them." Matthew 19:14

James and John Want to Be First

James and John were brothers. They were also two of Jesus' twelve disciples.

One day James and John said, "Jesus, we want you to do anything we ask."

Jesus knew what James and John were thinking. Still, he asked, "What do you want me to do for you?"

They spoke up boldly and said, "Make us your most important disciples. We want to be more important than everyone except you and your Father."

When the other disciples heard that James and John had asked Jesus to make them the most important disciples, they got angry!

Jesus knew all the selfish thoughts his disciples were thinking. He knew how wrong they were and that they needed to learn the right way to think about themselves.

Jesus said, "Some people try to be important by telling others what to do. They want to be first, and be in the most important place. These people act as if they were kings.

"But God wants you to treat the people around you as more important than yourself. You must happily serve others by being helpful and kind."

To Remember

Jesus sat down and called for the Twelve to come to him. Then he said, "If you want to be first, you must be the very last. You must be the servant of everyone."   Mark 9:35

Jesus Calls Zacchaeus

People crowded the streets of town. Jesus was coming, and everyone wanted to see him. Zacchaeus wanted to see Jesus, too. But Zacchaeus was too short and to see over the crowd.

Zacchaeus probably asked the people in front of him if they would let him move to the front so he could see, but no one would. Everyone knew Zacchaeus, and no one liked him.

Zacchaeus was a tax collector, and nobody liked tax collectors! People were certain Zacchaeus cheated them by collecting more tax money than the law required. Everyone knew Zacchaeus was rich, and they thought he was rich because he collected too much tax money and kept the extra for himself.

Zacchaeus really wanted to see Jesus, and suddenly, he had an idea! He ran to a big sycamore tree and climbed up into its branches. Now he was high above the people so he could see Jesus when he walked by.

Very soon Zacchaeus could see Jesus and the crowd of people coming down the road. When Jesus came to the tree, he stopped and looked up at Zacchaeus. Jesus said, "Zacchaeus, come down immediately. I must stay at your house today."

Zacchaeus was surprised! No one ever wanted to go to his house. Jesus knew Zacchaeus cheated people by collecting too much tax money, but Jesus still loved him.

Jesus went home with Zacchaeus. They ate a meal and talked like friends. Zacchaeus felt sorry for cheating people and told Jesus he would help poor people and pay back everyone he had cheated.

Jesus loved showed love to Zacchaeus, and Zacchaeus showed love to others.

To Remember

The Lord has been so good to me! How can I ever pay him back?   Psalm 116:12

The Most Important Rule

A crowd of people stood around Jesus. People were asking him questions. Some of the people in the crowd didn't like him. They knew Jesus taught the truth about God. They didn't like to hear the truth because they didn't want to follow it. These people who didn't like Jesus asked questions to trick him into saying something wrong about God. Jesus knew they were trying to trick him, but he still gave good answers that taught the truth about God.

One man thought he had a tricky question that Jesus would get wrong. "I have a question," he called out. "What's the most important rule?" The man knew there were more than 600 rules to follow. How would Jesus be able to pick the most important one?

Jesus said, "The most important rule is 'Love the Lord your God with all your heart and with all your soul and with all your mind and with all your strength.'"

The people knew this rule because it is in God's Word.

Then Jesus added, "The second most important rule is 'Love your neighbor as yourself.'"

The people knew this rule too because it is in God's Word.

The people in the crowd stopped asking Jesus tricky questions. They could tell Jesus knew what God wanted them to do.

To Remember

Jesus replied, "'Love the Lord your God with all your heart and with all your soul. Love him with all your mind.' This is the first and most important commandment." Matthew 22:37

Jesus Serves by Washing Feet

It was just before the Passover, and Jesus and the disciples were together for dinner.

Jesus got up from the meal and took off his outer clothes. He wrapped a towel around his waist like an apron. He poured water into a large bowl and started washing the disciples' feet.

When he came to Simon Peter, Peter said, "Lord, how can I let you wash my feet? That's a servant's job!"

Jesus said, "It doesn't make sense to you now, Peter, but what I'm doing is important. Later you'll understand."

"No," said Peter. "I will never let you wash my feet."

Jesus wanted Peter to understand. He said, "Unless you let me wash your feet, you can't share life with me."

Peter told Jesus, "In that case, wash my feet, my hands, all of me from head to foot."

"Peter, only your feet need to be washed right now."

When Jesus had finished washing their feet, he asked the disciples, "Do you understand why I washed your feet? I am both Teacher and Lord to you. So, if I love you

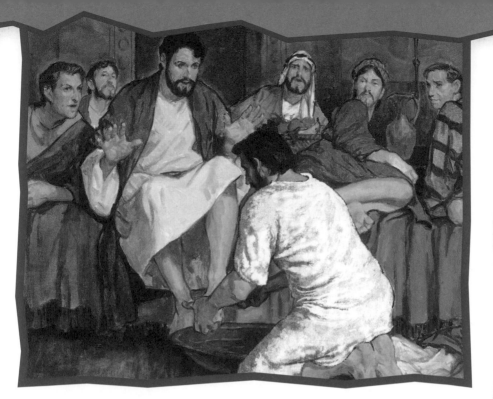

enough to wash your feet, shouldn't you love each other
enough to do the same? This is important," Jesus said.
"No matter who you are or how important you become,
don't forget to show love."

T͜o Remember

If you love one another, everyone will know
you are my disciples.   John 13:35

Jesus Dies

It was a sad day for the people who loved Jesus. Pilate, a Roman leader, said Jesus had to die on a cross.

The soldiers led Jesus up a hill. There they nailed his hands and feet to the cross. It must have hurt more than anything, but Jesus didn't cry or yell. He prayed. He said, "Father, forgive them. They don't know what they are doing."

Jesus' mother, Mary, other women, and John, the disciple, stood nearby. Jesus loved his mother and his friends, so he told John to take care of Mary.

At noon, Jesus was ready to die. Suddenly the sky grew dark. It seemed like midnight

instead of noon! Jesus prayed again, saying, "Father, into your hands I commit my very life." Then he died. Jesus knew he was doing God's work by dying, even though he didn't deserve any punishment. And now he had finished his part of God's work.

At the very moment Jesus took his last breath, the earth shook and split open. Even rocks broke apart.

The curtain in the most holy room of God's temple tore in half from top to bottom. Before Jesus died, ordinary people couldn't go to that room to be near God. But the curtain tore in two, and now God's people can be close to him anywhere, anytime.

Joseph, one of Jesus' friends, and Nicodemus, the man who had visited Jesus at night, took Jesus' body off the cross. They wrapped it in cloth and put Jesus' body in a tomb. (A tomb is a cave for burying dead people.) A big stone next to the cave would be rolled in front of the opening.

Some women who were friends of Jesus watched as

Joseph put Jesus' body in the tomb. Once the big rock was moved over the opening so the tomb was closed, Joseph and the women went to their homes.

All this happened on a Friday before the sun went down.

To Remember

We know what love is because Jesus Christ gave his life for us.   1 John 3:16

Jesus Comes Back to Life!

Saturday was the Sabbath. It was the one day of each week set aside to rest and worship God. All day Saturday, no one went to the tomb where Jesus was buried.

As the sun was coming up on Sunday morning, the women took spices and perfume to Jesus' tomb. In those days, people put spices and perfume on dead bodies both before and after they buried them. The women might have planned to ask some people to help them move the stone so they could go inside the tomb.

When the women arrived at the tomb, they had a big surprise. The stone was already moved away. They went into the tomb, but Jesus was not there! They didn't know what had happened to Jesus' body.

Suddenly, two angels stood beside the women. The women were afraid. The angels said to the women, "Jesus is alive! He is not here! He has risen! Remember how he told you he would be raised from the dead." Now the women remembered how Jesus had said he would die on a cross and be raised to life again.

The women went to tell the disciples what they had seen and heard. At first the disciples didn't believe Jesus was alive. One of the disciples, Peter, ran to the tomb to find out for himself. Peter saw the tomb was empty. He wondered what had happened to Jesus.

Later, Peter saw Jesus. Then Peter believed that Jesus was truly alive. The women were right. Jesus was

alive. Soon the other disciples, the women, and others saw Jesus too. They all believed that Jesus was now alive again.

Jesus died so God could show his power and bring him back to life. God is more powerful than anything, including death. When Jesus died and rose, he made a way for us to know God so we can live forever too.

Did You Know?

Jesus had told his friends that God was going to bring him back to life, but they didn't understand what he was telling them. That's why God sent an angel to explain what had happened. Then Jesus himself came to his friends to show them that he was with them again.

To Remember

We have been made holy because Jesus Christ offered his body once and for all time.

Hebrews 10:10

Two Friends Meet a Stranger

Two friends were walking home from Jerusalem and talking about how Jesus died. Another man caught up to walk with them. They thought he was just some stranger who wanted company on his journey. But it was no stranger. It was Jesus!

Jesus asked, "What are you talking about?"

One answered, "You must be a visitor from far away. Everyone who lives around here knows what happened."

They sadly told their visitor how Jesus had died. They explained about the women who went to the tomb and discovered it was empty.

Jesus explained what the Old Testament part of the Bible said about him. Jesus wanted the two friends to

know about him. But the two still didn't know their visitor was Jesus!

When they got home, the two said to their visitor, "It's getting late. Stay with us." So Jesus stayed.

The two friends fixed a meal. Jesus took the bread and prayed for the meal. Suddenly, the two friends both knew who their visitor was! Then Jesus suddenly left.

"That was Jesus!" the friends said. "He walked and talked with us so we would know he is alive!"

The two friends hurried back to Jerusalem to tell the disciples they knew Jesus had come alive again.

To Remember

Let us keep looking to Jesus. He is the author of faith.   Hebrews 12:2

Jesus Appears to Thomas

The night after Jesus rose from the dead, he came to see the disciples. He said, "May peace be with you!" Jesus' friends were so happy to see him!

But Thomas was not there.

The other disciples said to Thomas, "We have seen the Lord!" But Thomas couldn't believe Jesus was really alive. He said he wanted to see Jesus' hands and feet before he would believe.

About a week later, Thomas had his chance. Jesus appeared in the room—even though the doors were shut and locked tight! Thomas and his friends were there.

Again Jesus said, "May peace be with you!" Then Jesus called Thomas by name. He said, "Put your finger here. See my hands. Reach out your hand and put it into my side. Stop doubting and believe."

Thomas said, "My Lord and my God."

"Because you have seen me," Jesus said to Thomas, "you have believed. Blessed are those who have not seen me but still have believed."

To Remember

Blessed are those who have not seen me but still have believed.   John 20:29

Jesus Takes Peter Back

Before Jesus died, he knew what would happen. At his last meal with his disciples, he said, "All of you will turn away from me."

Peter said, "I will never turn away from you."

Jesus said, "Peter, three times you will say you don't even know me. It will happen tonight before the rooster crows."

Later that night, Jesus was taken by soldiers. Peter followed Jesus and sat outside the house. He knew Jesus was in trouble. Peter was afraid he might be in trouble too.

A servant girl said, "You were with Jesus."

Peter said, "I don't know what you're talking about."

Another girl said Peter was with Jesus.

Peter said, "I don't even know Jesus!"

Later some people said, "You are one of Jesus' followers. You talk like them."

Peter said, "I told you I don't know him!"

Just then a rooster crowed. Peter remembered what Jesus had said. Peter felt terrible. He went outside and cried.

One night after Jesus came alive again, Peter and some other disciples went fishing. John saw Jesus standing on the shore! He said, "It is the Lord!"

As soon as Peter heard that, he jumped into the water and swam to shore.

After breakfast, Jesus talked to Peter. Jesus reminded Peter that he loved him. Jesus gave Peter a special job. Jesus forgave Peter and welcomed him back.

To Remember

The Lord is gracious. He is kind and tender. He is slow to get angry. He is full of love.
Psalm 145:8

Prayer Point

Peter was a strong person, but even he was afraid sometimes. When Peter saw how Jesus was being treated, for a
while he forgot who Jesus was. But Peter admitted his
mistake and asked for forgiveness. Jesus forgave Peter.
Thank you, God, for showing us Peter's weakness. Thank
you for forgiving Peter, and thank you for forgiving us.

Luke 24;
Acts 1;
Romans 8

Jesus Returns to Heaven

After Jesus came back to life, he was with his disciples for forty days.

One day, Jesus ate with them and commanded them not to leave Jerusalem. He said, "Wait for the gift God has promised. In a few days you will be baptized by the Holy Spirit."

On the last day Jesus was on earth, he went walking with his disciples. They went up on a hill outside Jerusalem.

Jesus gathered his disciples around him. Then he blessed them. Jesus blessed his disciples so they would

know that he loved them then, and that he would always love them. Then he told them what he wanted them to do.

Jesus said, "You will receive power when the Holy Spirit comes. I want you to tell people everywhere about me and my love for them. Go and make disciples of all nations. Teach them to obey everything I have command-ed you. And you can be sure that I am always with you, to the very end."

While Jesus was talking with his disciples, he started going up into the sky!

The disciples looked up into the sky to see Jesus leave. They watched with wonder as he went up into the clouds. Even after they couldn't see Jesus anymore, the disciples still looked up.

Suddenly two angels appeared. They said, "Why are you looking at the sky? Jesus went back to heaven, but

he will come back someday in the same way you saw him go."

The disciples understood where Jesus went. They knew he is God's Son and that he went back to be with his Father in heaven.

The disciples were so excited about Jesus and his love for them that they ran back to Jerusalem and went to the temple to worship God and meet together.

After some days the disciples began telling people in Jerusalem about Jesus and his love. Then some of the disciples and other people who believed in Jesus started traveling to towns and cities in Israel and outside of Israel telling people about Jesus. They wanted everyone to know that Jesus always loves us.

TO REMEMBER

How did God show his love for us? He sent his one and only Son into the world. He sent him so we could receive life through him.

1 John 4:9

The Holy Spirit Comes

Thousands of people crowded the streets of Jerusalem. It was the Feast of Pentecost, and visitors from all over the world were there.

Jesus' friends and disciples had all gathered in one place.

Suddenly they heard a sound like a strong, rushing wind that filled the whole house. Then they saw flames of fire that settled on each person there.

At that moment, they were filled with the Holy Spirit, and they started talking in languages they'd never spoken before! The Holy Spirit gave them this ability. The crowd outside heard the noise, and they became con-

fused. They said, "Aren't all these men from Galilee?" We're from all over the world, so how is it we can understand them? They're talking about God's wonders in our languages!"

Some people just thought the believers were drunk. They made fun of the disciples.

Peter spoke to the crowd. He said, "Friends, these people aren't drunk. It's only nine o'clock in the morning! Listen to what I have to say."

Peter told the crowd about Jesus' death and resurrection. He said, "God raised Jesus from the dead and gave him a seat right next to his Father in heaven. God made Jesus the Lord!"

Everyone understood what he was saying and felt ashamed. They asked Peter, "What should we do? Peter answered, "You must turn away from your sins and be baptized in the name of Jesus. Then your sins will be for-

given. You will receive the gift of the Holy Spirit."

As a result of Peter's message, about three thousand people believed in Jesus and were baptized that day!

When the feast was over, the believers studied God's word and the disciples' teaching together. They ate together, and they prayed together. They all knew God was with them.

The believers even shared everything they had with each other and made sure everyone had what they needed.

They praised God together with honest and glad hearts. They were respected by all the people around them.

Every day more and more people trusted in Jesus and became part of this group of believers. God's family just kept growing!

Peter and James Heal a Lame Man

Peter and John were going to the temple. At the gate of the temple sat a beggar. He could not walk. So he could not work and earn money.

"Please give me some money," said the beggar to Peter and John.

Peter answered, "I don't have any money. But I will give you what I have. In Jesus' name, get up and walk!"

Peter took the man's hand and helped him get up. All of a sudden, the man's legs were strong! His feet were strong too. He stood up and walked for the first time in his life!

The man went into the temple. He was so happy he jumped for joy and praised God.

Many people came running. They saw the man walking.

"Isn't that the beggar?" they asked. "He's walking! How can this be?"

Peter spoke to the people. "Jesus gave us the power

to heal this man. Jesus is the Savior God promised to
send. He died for our sins. Then he rose from the dead. If
you believe in Jesus, he will forgive your sins."

Peter and John wanted to tell everyone about Jesus.

To Remember

They never stopped telling the good news that
Jesus is the Christ.   Acts 5:42

Paul Meets Jesus

Saul did not believe in Jesus, and he hated people who did. One day he set out for Damascus to find some of Jesus' friends. Saul was going to put them in jail.

Suddenly Saul saw a bright light. He fell to the ground.

A voice said, "Saul! Saul! Why are you attacking me?"

"Who are you, Lord?" asked Saul.

"I am Jesus. I am the one you are attacking. Now go into the city. When you get there, you'll be told what to do."

The men traveling with Saul stood still without speaking. They had heard the sound, but they didn't see anyone.

When Saul got up, he opened his eyes, but he couldn't see. His friends led him by the hand to Damascus.

Saul was blind for three days.

A man in Damascus named Ananias loved Jesus. Jesus told Ananias in a vision to go help Saul.

Ananias had heard about the bad things Saul had

done to people who loved Jesus. He didn't really want to help the man who had hurt his friends.

But the Lord said, "Go! I have chosen this man to work for me."

So Ananias obeyed. He went to the house where Saul was staying. Ananias put his hands on Saul's eyes. He said, "Brother Saul, you saw the Lord Jesus on the road as you were coming here. He has sent me so that you will be able to see again. You will be filled with the Holy Spirit."

At that moment something like scales fell from Saul's eyes. Right away he could see again.

Believing in Jesus changed Saul. He started telling people how Jesus had saved him. Saul was also called Paul.

Who Was That?

Saul was a teacher and a very important man. When Jesus' followers wouldn't stop talking about the things Jesus said, Saul was angry. He hated the Christians and wanted to punish all of them. But when he became a follower of Jesus, he changed his name to Paul. Then God used Paul in a big way to spread the word about Jesus. God will use us, too, if we are willing.

To Remember

Choose for yourselves right now whom you will serve.   Joshua 24:15

Paul Escapes in a Basket

Paul had just met Jesus in the light on the Damascus Road. He believed in Jesus and couldn't wait to tell everyone about the Lord. This was too important to keep to himself.

Hurrying to the synagogues, Paul began to preach. He boldly said that Jesus is the Son of God.

People couldn't believe what they were hearing. Paul had been so against the Christians before. How could he have changed?

"Isn't he the man who caused great trouble here in Jerusalem for those who worship Jesus?" they asked. "Hasn't he come here to take them as prisoners to the chief priests?"

But Paul just kept teaching. God blessed him, and many people listened and believed. Paul showed them that Jesus is God's Son.

The Jews in Damascus grew very worried. They didn't

want people to believe in Jesus. At a meeting one night, they came up with a plan.

They decided that Paul had to die.

But God wouldn't let Paul be harmed. There was still so much for Paul to do!

So Paul heard about the plan. Escape seemed impossible, but he had to find a way.

The city was surrounded by a wall. The gates were guarded. All day and night people watched for Paul to try leaving through the gates. If they saw him, he would die!

He had to find another way out.

Paul's friends had an idea. A large crack high in the

wall might be the answer. You could see outside the city through it. No one would expect Paul to leave that way.

Late one night, when it was dark, Paul's friends tied a big basket to a strong rope.

They helped Paul into the basket and carefully lowered him to the ground. No one heard or saw him leave.

Even when it seemed impossible, God kept Paul safe.

To Remember

He will cover you with his wings. Under the feathers of his wings you will find safety. He is faithful. He will keep you safe like a shield or tower.   Psalm 91:4

Peter Helps Dorcas

Acts 9

Dorcas made clothes for people who didn't have enough money to buy clothes. Many people depended on her help.

One day, Dorcas became sick and died. The people she had helped were very sad.

Some people sent two messengers to a nearby town where Peter was staying. The messengers said, "We need

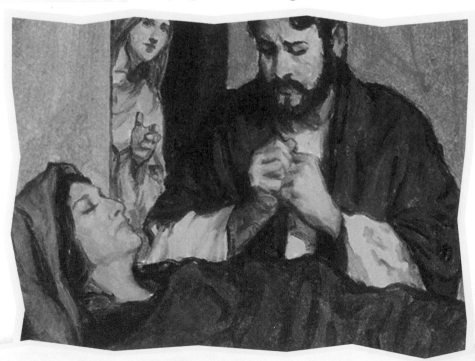

your help. Please come at once!"

The messengers led Peter to the room where Dorcas's body was. Many people were in the room too. They were crying because they missed Dorcas.

Peter asked all the people to leave the room. Then he got down on his knees next to Dorcas. Peter asked God to make Dorcas come alive again.

When Peter was done praying, he said, "Dorcas, get up." Immediately Dorcas opened her eyes and saw Peter.

Then Peter helped Dorcas stand up. Peter opened the door and called the people into the room to see Dorcas.

People all around the town heard how God made Dorcas alive again. Many people believed in Jesus because of what God did.

Did You Know?

Many of Jesus' followers were able to do the same miracles Jesus had done. They could make sick people well, make blind people see, and even bring people back to life. Many people started to believe in Jesus when they saw the miracles that Peter and the other followers did.

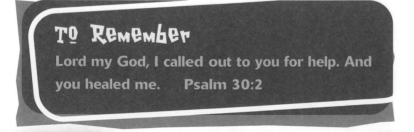

To Remember

Lord my God, I called out to you for help. And you healed me.   Psalm 30:2

Barnabas and Paul Work Together

People in a town called Antioch learned the good news about Jesus. People in Antioch trusted Jesus and followed him.

Others noticed how these people followed Christ, so they called these believers "Christians." The word *Christian* means "Christ follower."

The Christians in Antioch wanted to know more about Jesus, but they didn't have anyone to teach them.

Some of the believers in Jerusalem learned about the Christians in Antioch who needed someone to teach them. The believers in Jerusalem sent a man named Barnabas to Antioch.

When he arrived, Barnabas could see that the people believed in Jesus by the way they lived. He knew why they were called Christians. They really did follow Jesus.

Barnabas stayed to teach and encourage the people. More and more people came to learn from him. Soon there were too many for him to teach alone. Barnabas needed someone to work with him to teach the people.

Barnabas knew Paul, so he traveled to the town where Paul lived. He found Paul and said, "Please come work with me in Antioch." Paul was willing, so they went back to Antioch to teach the Christians there about Jesus. Barnabas and Paul worked together telling people the good news about Jesus for a whole year.

To Remember

Two people are better than one. They can help each other in everything they do.

Ecclesiastes 4:9

An Angel Frees Peter

Peter was in jail! King Herod had locked him up just because Peter loved Jesus.

Herod wanted to be sure Peter couldn't get away. He had four soldiers guarding Peter all the time. The guards put a chain around each of Peter's wrists. The end of each chain was locked to a guard. Then outside the jail door stood two more guards. It seemed like Peter was pretty well locked up. Peter was pretty sure he wasn't going anywhere, so he lay down and slept.

God's people knew Peter was locked in jail. They wanted to help him, but they weren't sure how. So God's people gathered at a house to pray that God would help Peter.

That night while Peter slept, an angel came and stood next to him. Peter must have been sleeping soundly! He didn't wake up until the angel tapped him hard and said, "Get up quickly!" The chains fell from Peter's hands.

The angel told Peter to follow him, so Peter walked behind the angel right past the guards standing outside

the jail cell! At first, Peter thought he was dreaming. But
as Peter and the angel walked down the city street leading from Herod's jail, Peter began to realize what had
happened. Then the angel left.

Now Peter was wide awake. He knew then that he
wasn't dreaming. God had rescued him from jail.

Peter hurried to his friends' house, where people were praying.

Knock, knock. A young girl named Rhoda, who worked at the house, came to the door. "It's me! Peter!" said Peter as he knocked. Rhoda was so surprised to hear Peter's voice she forgot to open the door! Instead, she ran back to the room where the people were praying. "Peter is here! He's at the door!" Rhoda said.

But the people said, "That can't be true. Peter is in jail."

Knock, knock. Peter kept knocking at the door. Finally Rhoda opened the door. "Peter! It is Peter!" they all cried.

Peter told God's people about how God had sent an angel to get him out of jail. The people were so excited and happy that Peter was safe. God answered when his people prayed for each other.

To Remember

Lord, you hear the longings of those who are hurting. You cheer them up and give them hope. You listen to their cries.

Psalm 10:17

Paul and Silas Sing in Jail

One day, Paul and Silas cast out a demon from a slave girl who had been following them.

The owners of the girl got mad. They liked having a slave with a demon. The demon could make the girl tell the future, and people paid the owners money to hear their futures. The angry owners dragged Paul and Silas to the city judge.

The judge didn't like Paul and Silas, so he let the guards beat them with sticks.

Then a jailer locked Paul and Silas in a cell. He wanted to make sure they couldn't run away, so he put their feet in stocks, which are thick wooden blocks that keep a person from moving around at all.

Paul and Silas didn't care about the cuts and bruises or the stocks. They didn't mind being in jail. They trusted God and sang songs about how wonderful God is. The other prisoners listened as Paul and Silas sang.

About midnight, an earthquake shook the jail. All the doors flew open, and the locks on the stocks came off!

The jailer heard the earthquake and thought all the prisoners had escaped. He knew he was going to be in big trouble, so he drew his sword and placed the sharp tip right against his skin.

"Wait!" Paul shouted. "We're all here!"

When he heard Paul, the jailer was so happy! He fell down in front of Paul and Silas and asked, "What must I do to be saved?"

Paul answered, "Believe in the Lord Jesus. Then you and your family will be saved."

The jailer took Paul and Silas to his house, cleaned their cuts and bruises, and gave them something to eat. He and his whole family were filled with joy. They had become believers in God!

To Remember

You are my hiding place. You will keep me safe from trouble. You will surround me with songs sung by those you praise you because you save your people. Psalm 32:7

Timothy's Family Helps Him Know God

Timothy was a happy little boy. Timothy's mother was named Eunice. She wanted him to know about God. So, from the time Timothy was very little, she read God's Word to him so he would know God. Timothy was a good listener and learned about God. He learned God's laws and the powerful things God did to help his people know about his great love. Little Timothy learned to love God and his Word.

Timothy's grandmother also lived with the family. Her name was Lois. She spent a lot of time with Timothy. Grandmother Lois also loved God very much. Timothy would listen when she talked about God.

Time went by and Timothy became a young man. Now Timothy was able to read God's Word for himself.

One day Paul came to the town where Timothy and his family lived. Paul taught crowds of people about God's Son, Jesus. Timothy and his mother and grandmother listened to Paul teach about Jesus. They understood what Paul taught because they knew God's Word very well.

Later, Paul made another trip back to Timothy's town. Paul came to tell more people about Jesus and look for a helper. Paul needed someone who could work with him teaching others about Jesus. Paul asked Timothy to help tell people about Jesus.

Timothy was excited that Paul asked him to help teach people about Jesus. Timothy had learned about God and his Word from his family. Now Timothy would help others to know about God and his Son Jesus. Timothy knew he could serve others by teaching them from God's Word.

Timothy left home with Paul to go to other towns to teach people about Jesus. Timothy was glad his family helped him know God.

To Remember

You have known the Holy Scriptures ever since you were a little child. They are able to teach you how to be saved by believing in Christ Jesus.   2 Timothy 3:15

Who Was That?

Timothy was a young man who became a follower of Jesus. He made friends with Paul. Paul helped Timothy to become a preacher of Jesus just like he was. Timothy loved Paul and he loved Jesus.

Paul Helps People Know God

Paul went to Athens, where he found a city full of statues of false gods. He spoke to the people in a synagogue, in the marketplace, and finally, in the city meeting hall.

The people there didn't know about the true God. They had never heard the good news about Jesus, either.

They came to Paul and said, "You have some strange ideas. We've never heard them before. We want to know what they mean."

Paul was happy to tell them about God and his Son Jesus. He saw that they needed to hear the truth.

"As I walked around, I looked carefully at the things you worship. I even found an altar with 'TO AN UNKNOWN GOD' written on it."

Paul told the people how God had made the world and everything in it. He told them that God doesn't want people to make idols of him.

When Paul talked about how God raised Jesus from the dead, some people laughed and made fun of Paul. Others asked to hear more later. But best of all, a few men and women believed the truth about Jesus and became Christians.

To Remember

You can't be saved by believing in anyone else. God has given us no other name under heaven that will save us.   Acts 4:12

New Friends Learn About Jesus

Paul traveled from town to town telling people about God and his Son Jesus. In Corinth, he met Aquila and his wife, Priscilla. They soon became friends. Paul learned that Aquila and Priscilla believed in Jesus. Paul made tents to earn money, just like Aquila and Priscilla did. Aquila and Priscilla invited Paul to stay with them and work with them making tents. So he did.

While the three of them worked together, they talked about Jesus. There were things Aquila and Priscilla didn't know, so Paul helped them learn more about Jesus.

When the time came for Paul to leave Corinth, he and Aquila and Priscilla sailed to Ephesus. Paul didn't stay there long, but his friends did. Aquila and Priscilla stayed in Ephesus to make and sell tents, and tell more people about Jesus.

While Aquila and Priscilla were in Ephesus, they met Apollos and became friends with him. Apollos loved and worshipped God too. He was also a very good preacher. However, Apollos didn't know that Jesus died for our sins and then went back to heaven to be with his Father.

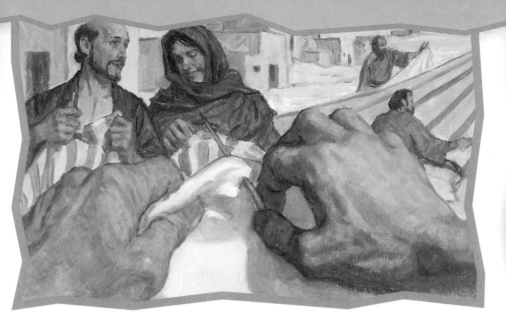

Aquila and Priscilla invited Apollos to their home. They told their new friend more about Jesus. Now Apollos was able to teach people much more.

Aquila and Priscilla learned more about Jesus because of all their new friend Paul told them. Apollos learned more about Jesus from his new friends Aquila and Priscilla.

To Remember

All over the world the good news is bearing fruit and growing. It has been doing that among you since the day you heard it.

Colossians 1:6

Paul Cares for the Church

Paul cared for God's people by teaching them what they needed to know about following Jesus.

Some of the people learned so well from Paul that they also became leaders of the church. Paul was glad for these new leaders who were beginning to care for the church with him. He spent time with these leaders, helping them learn how to care for God's people.

One day, Paul asked the new leaders of the church in Ephesus to meet him at the beach. Only Paul knew why they were gathering there.

When they met, Paul told the new church leaders how he used every opportunity to tell people about Jesus and encourage people everywhere to ask Jesus to forgive their sins. Paul told the people these things to encourage them to be caring leaders like he was.

Then Paul told the leaders what God wanted him to do next. He knew God wanted him to go to Jerusalem to be with the Christians there. In fact, he explained that he needed to get on a ship in a few minutes. Paul said he would never again see the people on the beach.

This was not what the new leaders wanted! The people in the church loved Paul. And Paul loved them.

Before Paul left, he and the leaders prayed together one last time. They cried and hugged each other. Then the men watched Paul get on the ship. They knew God wanted Paul to lead the Christians in Jerusalem. And God wanted them to lead the Christians in their town caring for God's people and using everything Paul had taught them.

To Remember

[Paul said,] "I commit you to God's care. I commit you to the word of his grace. It can build you up." Acts 20:32

Paul's Ship Sinks

Paul had gotten into a lot of trouble for telling people about Jesus. Now he was a prisoner. He had to sail to Rome to let the leaders decide what should happen next. On the ship, a Roman commander named Julius made sure Paul, and the other prisoners, didn't escape.

While they were sailing, a huge storm blew in. The wind was so strong that the sailors had to tie ropes around the ship to keep it from breaking apart.

The storm went on and on. No one could see the sun or stars for days. The sailors threw everything they could overboard to make the ship lighter and keep it from sinking.

One night, an angel came to Paul and told him no one would die in the storm as long as everyone stayed with the ship. This cheered up everyone.

Finally they put Paul on a boat to Rome. The boat got into a terrible storm and crashed.

Finally, the ship reached shallow water, and some sailors tried to escape in the lifeboat. Paul warned Julius and his soldiers they wouldn't live if these men didn't stay with the ship, so the soldiers cut the lifeboat's ropes.

After two weeks in the storm, the sailors saw a sandy beach and steered the ship toward it. But the ship got stuck on a sandbar, and began to break apart.

The soldiers wanted to kill the prisoners to keep them from swimming away and escaping. But Julius stepped in and ordered everyone to swim to shore.

Just like God promised, all the people got to shore safely.

To Remember

The Lord himself will go ahead of you. He will be with you. He will never leave you. He'll never desert you.

Deuteronomy 31:8

Did You Know?

Traveling in Paul's day was very different from how it is today. There were no airplanes, so sometimes people had to travel by boat. It was not always safe to travel by boat. Big storms could come and blow the ship into rocks. Three times when Paul was on a boat trip, the boat he was on was wrecked. But God took good care of Paul even when the boat wasn't strong enough. God will take care of us too, if we ask him.

Paul Teaches About Giving

Some people in Jerusalem who loved Jesus were having hard times. They were hungry because there wasn't enough food in the crowded city. Other people couldn't get jobs to make money. Since people couldn't get work, they didn't have money to buy food.

Paul knew about the problems in Jerusalem. When he visited other towns, he told how those in Jerusalem needed help. Paul taught the people to give money to their church to send to Christians in Jerusalem.

Many people listened and obeyed. They cheerfully set money aside to give. Some were very poor. They didn't even have enough for themselves. But because they loved God, they wanted to give all they could.

Paul sent letters to the people who went to church in the city of Corinth. He said, "Collect the money you want to give. You shouldn't give if you don't want to. No one is forcing you to give. Remember all God has given you, then gladly give what you want. God loves a cheerful giver."

Paul continued traveling to visit the people who were collecting money to give to those in need in Jerusalem. In each city and town the people handed to Paul the money they had collected. Paul and other men took the money to the people in Jerusalem.

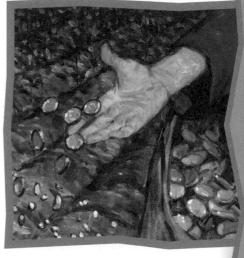

When Paul and the men arrived in Jerusalem with the money, the people were excited to see them. Paul said, "Many people knew that you didn't have money to buy food. They gave cheerfully out of love. We are pleased to bring their money to give to you. Now you can buy food and other things you need."

The people in Jerusalem were so happy. They thanked Paul and the others who brought the money, and they thanked God. The people in Jerusalem knew people in other towns loved them.

To Remember

Let us not become tired of doing good. At the right time we will gather a crop if we don't give up. So when we can do good to everyone, let us do it.
Galatians 6:9-10

Onesimus Comes Home

Onesimus did not like being a slave. He worked for a man named Philemon. One day Onesimus did something wrong. He ran away from Philemon.

Onesimus headed for the best place he knew to hide: the big city of Rome.

There Onesimus met Paul, who was a friend of Philemon. Paul told Onesimus about Jesus. Onesimus believed in Jesus.

Now he was sorry for the wrong things he'd done, especially for running away. He wanted to go back home.

Paul sent a letter to his friend Philemon.

Dear Philemon,
Your slave Onesimus has become a believer in Jesus! He has helped me while I've been in jail for talking about Jesus. In fact, he's become like a son to me. Because we're all believers in Jesus, I want you to welcome him back. I hope to see you soon.

Your friend,
Paul

TO REMEMBER

The free gift of God's grace makes all of us right with him. Christ Jesus paid the price to set us free.   Romans 3:24

"To Remember" Verses

Genesis 1:3 11
Genesis 1:11 13
Genesis 1:25 16
Genesis 2:7 19
Genesis 2:16–17 21
Genesis 6:22 29
Genesis 9:17 31
Genesis 12:1–2 36
Genesis 15:5-6 45
Exodus 12:50 80
Exodus 15:13 84
Exodus 20:8 259
Exodus 20:12 95
Leviticus 22:31 211
Deuteronomy 8:6 77
Deuteronomy 31:8 402
Joshua 10:25 101
Joshua 24:15 . . . . .114, 373
1 Kings 8:56 147
Psalm 5:3 112
Psalm 9:10 294
Psalm 10:17 385
Psalm 14:6 177
Psalm 17:6 169
Psalm 29:2 133
Psalm 29:9 . . . . .182, 231
Psalm 30:2 379
Psalm 32:7 389
Psalm 34:14 53
Psalm 34:17 49
Psalm 37:3 197
Psalm 37:26 291

Psalm 37:30 141
Psalm 38:15 273
Psalm 51:10 24
Psalm 56:3 122
Psalm 66:4 199
Psalm 71:19 185
Psalm 85:3 93
Psalm 85:8 178
Psalm 86:9 229
Psalm 91:9 43
Psalm 95:3 151
Psalm 115:8 88
Psalm 116:12 339
Psalm 119:9 167
Psalm 119:33 202
Psalm 119:60 217
Psalm 119:89 191
Psalm 121:7 71
Psalm 139:1 269
Psalm 145:8 358
Proverbs 1:8 91
Proverbs 4:7 136
Proverbs 10:12 130
Proverbs 13:20 159
Proverbs 17:17 127
Proverbs 19:20 235
Ecclesiastes 4:9 381
Isaiah 6:3 189
Isaiah 26:4 47
Isaiah 33:15 59
Isaiah 55:8 108
Isaiah 57:18 262
Jeremiah 17:14 253
Daniel 4:34 64
Amos 5:1 207

Malachi 117
Matthew 4:19 249
Matthew 5:44 163
Matthew 6:33 320
Matthew 7:7 277
Matthew 19:14 335
Matthew 22:37 341
Matthew 25:40 309
Mark 9:23 296
Mark 9:35 337
Luke 1:37 214
Luke 2:11 221
Luke 2:14 225
Luke 4:18–19 245
Luke 5:31–32 257
Luke 11:2–5 311
Luke 12:34 279
Luke 15:10 329
Luke 19:10 324
John 1:29 238
John 3:16 265
John 8:12 313
John 10:14 316
John 11:25 333
John 13:35 343
John 20:29 355
Acts 2:42 367
Acts 4:12 395
Acts 5:42 369
Acts 20:32 399
Romans 3:24 407
Romans 10:6 287
Romans 12:18 41
1 Corinthians 10:13 242
1 Corinthians 10:31 193

2 Corinthians 9:7 . . . . .97, 172

2 Corinthians 12:9 73

Galatians 5:22–23 61

Galatians 6:9–10 405

Ephesians 2:10 305

Ephesians 4:25 55

Ephesians 4:32 69

Ephesians 6:10 120

Colossians 1:6 397

Colossians 3:13 301

1 Timothy 4:10 227

2 Timothy 3:15 393

Titus 3:1 303

Hebrews 7:27 144

Hebrews 10:10 350

Hebrews 12:2 353

Hebrews 13:6 105

James 1:22 282

1 Peter 5:7 154

1 John 3:16 347

1 John 4:9 363

Bible Story References

Genesis 1 (day and night) 10
Genesis 1 (plants) 12
Genesis 1 (animals) 14
Genesis 1–2 (people) 18
Genesis 3 20
Genesis 4 22
Genesis 6–7 26
Genesis 8–9 30
Genesis 12 34
Genesis 13 38
Genesis 15 44
Genesis 19 42
Genesis 21 44
Genesis 22 46
Genesis 24 48
Genesis 25 54
Genesis 26 50
Genesis 27 54
Genesis 27–28 56
Genesis 32–33 56
Genesis 37 . . . . 45, 60
Genesis 45 66
Genesis 39–41 62
Exodus 1–2 70
Exodus 3–4 72
Exodus 3–5 74
Exodus 12 . . . . 74, 78
Exodus 14 82
Exodus 17 86
Exodus 18 90
Exodus 19–20 94
Exodus 32 92

Exodus 35 96
Joshua 6. 98
Judges 6–7 102
Judges 7. 106
1 Samuel 1–2 110
1 Samuel 9. 114
1 Samuel 15. 116
1 Samuel 17. 118
1 Samuel 18. 122
1 Samuel 18–20 124
1 Samuel 26 128
2 Samuel 1 132
2 Samuel 5–6 132
1 Kings 3 (God's offer to Solomon) 134
1 Kings 3 (Solomon and two mothers) 138
1 Kings 5–6. 142
1 Kings 8 146
1 Kings 18 148
1 Kings 19 152
2 Kings 2 156
2 Kings 6 160
2 Kings 12 170
2 Kings 22–23 164
2 Chronicles 20. 168
2 Chronicles 29 174
Nehemiah 8. 146
Esther 1–10 178
Job 184
Isaiah 6. 186
Jeremiah 36. 190
Daniel 1 192
Daniel 3 194
Daniel 5 198
Daniel 6. 200
Amos 204

Jonah 1–3 208
Matthew 1 (Mary) 214
Matthew 1 (Joseph) 216
Matthew 2 (wise men) 228
Matthew 2 (flight to Egypt) 230
Matthew 3 236
Matthew 4 (temptation of Jesus) 240
Matthew 4 (miracle of fish) 246
Matthew 6 278
Matthew 7 (Jesus chooses disciples) 274
Matthew 7 (wise and foolish builders) 280
Matthew 9 254
Matthew 13 232
Matthew 14 292
Matthew 15 296
Matthew 18 298
Matthew 25 (parable of three servants) 304
Matthew 25 (sheep and goats) 306
Mark 1 (temptation of Jesus) 240
Mark 1 (Jesus heals a leper) 250
Mark 2 260
Mark 7 296
Mark 10 (Jesus and the children) 334
Mark 10 (who will be first) 336
Mark 12 340
Luke 1 214
Luke 2 (Jesus' birth) 218
Luke 2 (shepherds) 222
Luke 2 (Simeon) 226
Luke 2 (boy Jesus) 232
Luke 4 (temptation of Jesus) 240
Luke 4 (Jesus claims to be Messiah) 244
Luke 5 (miracle of fish) 246
Luke 5 (man through the roof) 260
Luke 5 (Jesus heals a leper) 250

Luke 6 (Jesus heals on the Sabbath) 258
Luke 6 (Jesus chooses disciples) 274
Luke 8 284
Luke 11 310
Luke 12 (do not worry) 278
Luke 12 (parable of the foolish rich man) 318
Luke 15 (parable of the lost sheep) 322
Luke 15 (parable of the prodigal son) 326
Luke 19 338
Luke 22 302
Luke 23 (Jesus' death) 344
Luke 23 (Jesus' resurrection) 348
Luke 24 (Emmaus road) 352
Luke 24 (Jesus' ascension) 360
John 1 236
John 3 264
John 4 266
John 5 270
John 6 288
John 9 312
John 10 314
John 11 330
John 13 342
John 17 274
John 19 344
John 20 354
John 21 356
Acts 1 (Jesus' ascension) 360
Acts 1–2 364
Acts 3 368
Acts 9 (Paul's conversion) 370
Acts 9 (Paul's escape) 374
Acts 9 (Dorcas) 378
Acts 11 380
Acts 12 382

Acts 13 374

Acts 16 (Paul and Silas in jail) 386

Acts 16 (Timothy) 390

Acts 17 394

Acts 18 396

Acts 20 398

Acts 27–28 400

Romans 8 360

1 Corinthians 15 348

1 Corinthians 16 404

2 Corinthians 8–9 404

2 Timothy 1, 3 390

Philemon 406